NORTH AMERICAN FIELD GUIDES

# POISONOUS AND DEADLY PLANTS

Rachel C. Hart

Field Guides

An Imprint of Abdo Reference | abdobooks.com

# CONTENTS

## Ornamental Flowers



## Ornamental Plants



## Pokeweeds



## Poppies



## Spurges



## Sumacs



## Thistles



## Vines



## Wetland Plants



## Yews



## Other Poisonous Plants

# WHAT ARE POISONOUS PLANTS?

A poisonous plant is any type of plant that may cause harm to humans or animals when touched or eaten. Some plants can cause irritation to the skin and eyes when handled. When ingested, or eaten, many species of plants can produce serious reactions. They can harm the digestive system, nervous system, or internal organs and brain. Some plants are considered deadly plants because ingesting them can be fatal.

Different parts of a plant can be poisonous. The berries, fruits, flowers, or seeds of some plants can be toxic. Other plants have toxic root systems, stems, leaves, or sap instead. Some species of plants only have a few poisonous parts. Other species are completely poisonous.

## SAFETY

It is very important to be extremely cautious. Never touch a plant unless you are 100 percent certain of its identity. This is because poisonous plants are very widespread and grow alongside harmless plants.

## WHAT ARE POISONOUS AND DEADLY PLANTS LIKE?

Poisonous plants can sometimes be difficult to identify because they share many traits with nonpoisonous plants. They have stem, leaf, and root systems. Many also produce colorful flowers and berries. Scientists theorize that poisonous plants developed their toxins as a survival defense mechanism. It helps them avoid being eaten.

Because poisonous plants can be dangerous, it is important to identify their distinguishing features. These depend on the plant. Sometimes the leaves, flowers, or berries are unique to the poisonous species. Other times it is important to look at the stems, seeds, or roots.

There is great variety in the forms different poisonous plants take. They come in all sizes, from tiny weeds to huge trees. Some are vines, while others are trees or shrubs. Still others are small flowering plants or weeds.

Poisonous and deadly plants can be found in many different environments throughout North America. They grow in deserts, wetlands, mountains, woodlands, and fields. Many also grow in disturbed areas, or areas where vegetation and topsoil have been removed through human activity. Certain poisonous species are even planted as decorations. They have beautiful flowers or leaves.

Some poisonous plants are invasive. They can damage the ecosystem and threaten biodiversity. Other poisonous plants can benefit the environment. They provide food for pollinators, such as the bees, birds, and butterflies who eat their nectar. Many also have uses in medicines and have been historically important amongst American Indian peoples.

# HOW TO USE THIS BOOK

Tab shows the poisonous and deadly plants category.

The plant's common name appears here.

CACTI

## PEYOTE CACTUS

*(LOPHOPHORA WILLIAMSII)*

The peyote cactus does not have spines. It has a rounded
t grows close to the ground. It has a distinctive
en color. This cactus grows in small clusters that
uttons or pincushions topped with small tufts
oles. During the day, the peyote cactus blooms
pink or white flowers on the top of its rounded
gesting it can cause hallucinations, vomiting,
dizziness, difficulty breathing, and increased blood pressure and heart rate.

This paragraph gives information about the plant.

**FUN FACT**

Peyote has cultural significance because American Indian peoples have used it for medicine and rituals for more than 5,500 years.

**HOW TO SPOT**

**Size:** 2 inches (5.1 cm) tall; up to 4 inches (10.2 cm) in diameter

**Flower:** Pink or white, 0.4 to 0.9 inches (1 to 2.3 cm) in diameter

**Habitat:** Dry desert areas

**Range:** Southwestern United States and Mexico

*Fun Facts* give interesting information about poisonous and deadly plants.

30

DY BEAR CACTUS

*NDROPUNTIA BIGELOVII)*

ddy bear, or cholla, cactus stands upright, with a thick hat branches at the top. Small yellow-green flowers at the tops of its stems. The teddy bear cactus gets nmon name because its stems are completely covered all spines, giving it a fuzzy look. However, these es are very sharp and painful to remove when they in the skin. These spikes are also the most dangerous of the plant. Although they are not poisonous, they can e skin irritation, injury, and infection.

OW TO SPOT

ize: 1 to 5 feet (0.3 to 5 m) tall

lower: Yellow-green, 4 inches (3.6 cm) long

Habitat: Desert areas with high elevations

Range: Southwestern United States and northwest Mexico

WHAT ARE CACTI?

Cactuses or cacti thrive in dry, desert areas where most other plants cannot grow. They are able to take water from the soil and store it inside their thick, fleshy, tough-skinned stems. Many cactus plants have sharp needles or spines around their stems, and they typically have no leaves.

31

The plant's scientific name appears here.

*How to Spot* features information about the plant's size, habitats, and range.

Images show the plant.

Sidebars provide additional information about the topic.

# APRICOT ANGEL'S TRUMPET

## *(BRUGMANSIA VERSICOLOR)*

The apricot angel's trumpet has large, drooping flowers that hang upside down. Their leaves sit above the plant's flower. The oval leaves have smooth edges. Their flowers are the largest of all angel's trumpets and change from white to an apricot color as they mature. The flowers, leaves, and seeds of the apricot angel's trumpet are poisonous when ingested. They cause hallucinations, muscle weakness, increased pulse and blood pressure, and potential paralysis.

### HOW TO SPOT

**Size:** 10 to 16 feet (3 to 4.9 m) tall

**Flower:** White to peach, 10 to 12 inches (25.4 to 30.5 cm) long

**Habitat:** Sloping terrain with moist soil

**Range:** Western United States and Mexico

## WHAT ARE ANGEL'S TRUMPETS?

Angel's trumpets can be shrubs or small trees. They thrive in warm, moist regions. Angel's trumpets are characterized by large, trumpet-shaped flowers that hang upside down. All parts of angel's trumpets are toxic to humans, pets, and livestock such as horses.

# GOLDEN ANGEL'S TRUMPET

## *(BRUGMANSIA AUREA)*

The leaves of the golden angel's trumpet are called untoothed because they have smooth edges. The flowers of the golden angel's trumpet are usually yellow or white. They may hang either downward, like those of other angel's trumpets, or point horizontally from the plant. Golden angel's trumpets are poisonous to humans and animals. Ingesting any part of them can cause intense hallucinations, seizures, and potentially death.

### HOW TO SPOT

**Size:** 10 to 20 feet (3 to 6.1 m) tall

**Flower:** Yellow or white, 10 to 16 inches (25.4 to 40.6 cm) long

**Habitat:** Sloping terrain with moist soil

**Range:** Western United States and Mexico

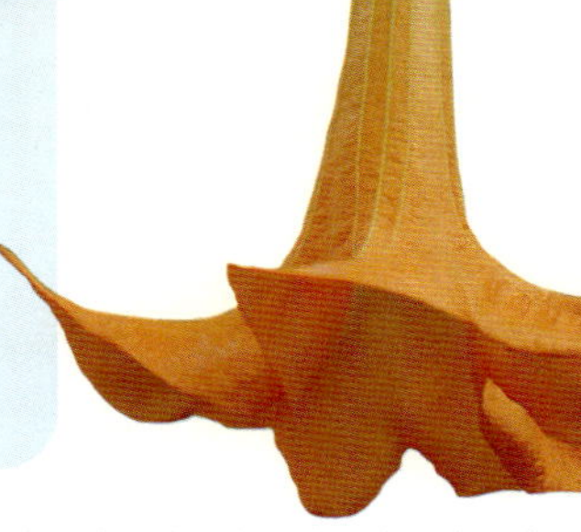

# RED ANGEL'S TRUMPET

## *(BRUGMANSIA SANGUINEA)*

The red angel's trumpet has the most vibrant flowers of the species. Its flowers hang upside down. The flowers have bright red mouths with yellow veins and sides and green bases. Their leaves are smooth-edged and oval-shaped. The flowers attract hummingbirds but do not have a strong fragrance. All parts of the plant are poisonous to humans, pets, and livestock. Ingesting them can cause confusion, seizures, or even death in some cases.

### HOW TO SPOT

**Size:** 10 to 16 feet (3 to 4.9 m) tall
**Flower:** Red, 12 inches (30.5 cm) long
**Habitat:** Mountainous areas
**Range:** Western United States and Mexico

# WHITE ANGEL'S TRUMPET

## *(BRUGMANSIA SUAVEOLENS)*

The white angel's trumpet has large, hanging flowers that are very fragrant. Colors range from white to pastel orange or pale pink. The trunks of white angel's trumpets often have several branches. Their large leaves are smooth and oval-shaped. Every part of the white angel's trumpet is poisonous. It can cause hallucinations, seizures, and death in some cases when ingested.

### HOW TO SPOT

**Size:** Up to 33 feet (10.1 m) tall
**Flower:** White, 9 to 13 inches (22.9 to 33 cm) long
**Habitat:** Sloping terrain with moist soil
**Range:** Western United States and Mexico

# DIEFFENBACHIA

## *(DIEFFENBACHIA SEGUINE)*

Dieffenbachia, commonly called dumb cane, has distinctive large leaves with vibrant color patterns. Their leaves are shaped like wide arrows with smooth edges. Their flowers have an upright white spadix surrounded by a green spathe that resembles an unfolding leaf. Dumb cane leaves contain needle-like crystals. When ingested, they can cause paralysis of the mouth, tongue, throat, and vocal cords. Touching the eyes after touching dumb cane leaves can result in swelling and temporary vision loss.

### HOW TO SPOT

**Size:** Up to 6 feet (1.8 m) tall

**Leaves:** Oval-shaped, pointed tips, smooth edges, and vibrant patterns, 18 inches (45.7 cm) long; 12 inches (30.5 cm) wide

**Habitat:** Coastal plains and woodlands

**Range:** United States and Mexico

## WHAT IS THE ARACEAE FAMILY OF PLANTS?

The Araceae family is a large family of flowering plants. Its many varieties of plants can look different and grow in different habitats. Many have unique blooms with a spadix and spathe. A spadix is an upright flower spike. A spathe is a kind of sheath that wraps around the spadix and covers it either completely or partially.

# EASTERN SKUNK CABBAGE

## *(SYMPLOCARPUS FOETIDUS)*

Eastern skunk cabbage gets its name because it produces a bad-smelling odor, like a skunk. This odor gets stronger over time, as the plant gets older. Its leaves are wide and oval-shaped with rounded ends. Its flowers are dark purple and spotted, with spathes shaped like shells or hoods surrounding a flowered spadix. Handling the eastern skunk cabbage can burn the skin, mouth, and throat. Eating this plant causes vomiting, dizziness, and headaches.

**FUN FACT**

Eastern skunk cabbage blooms when there is still snow on the ground, but it produces its own heat and can melt the ice immediately around it.

### HOW TO SPOT

**Size:** 2 to 3 feet (0.6 to 0.9 m) tall
**Flower:** Spotted purple spathe around a spadix 3 to 6 inches (7.6 to 15.2 cm) tall
**Habitat:** Woodlands and wetlands
**Range:** Eastern Canada and northeastern United States

# JACK-IN-THE-PULPIT

## *(ARISAEMA TRIPHYLLUM)*

The Jack-in-the-pulpit has a large, hooded flower. Its spathe, called the pulpit, looks like a green-and-purple-striped hood. It wraps around and over the upright, off-white spadix, called the Jack. These plants have three leaves on the top of the stem in a wide T shape. The leaves grow in a pointy arrow shape, and they have smooth edges and a prominent central vein. Touching Jack-in-the-pulpit can blister the skin, and eating any part of it raw can irritate the throat, respiratory system, and digestive tract.

### HOW TO SPOT

**Size:** 1 to 2 feet (0.3 to 0.6 m) tall

**Flower:** Green or striped spathe around a spadix, 3 to 4 inches (7.6 to 10.2 cm) tall

**Habitat:** Moist woodlands

**Range:** Eastern Canada and the eastern and southern United States

# POTHOS *(EPIPREMNUM AUREUM)*

Pothos is also known as golden pothos or devil's ivy. It is a climbing vine known for its abundant foliage. It can grow very long when it clings to trees for support. Pothos has distinctive large, waxy, heart-shaped leaves with a yellow marbled pattern. Pothos is toxic to cats and dogs and can cause vomiting, mouth irritation, and difficulty swallowing. In humans, it can cause skin irritation and burning and swelling of the mouth. Pothos is an invasive species.

## HOW TO SPOT

**Size:** Up to 40 feet (12.2 m) when climbing
**Leaves:** Waxy and heart-shaped, marble pattern, 4 to 28 inches (10.2 to 71.1 cm) long
**Habitat:** Moist, warm woodlands
**Range:** Southeastern United States

### FUN FACT

Pothos reportedly got the name *devil's ivy* because it is so difficult to kill.

# WATER ARUM *(CALLA PALUSTRIS)*

Water arum grows in shallow water. The heart-shaped leaves are smooth and waxy. They have pointed tips and edges that curve upward, like cups. Water arum flowers feature an oval, white spathe that partially covers a spiky, upright spadix packed with tiny, greenish yellow flowers. All parts of the water arum plant are poisonous. It causes intense pain in the lips, mouth, tongue, and throat and affects the ability to speak.

## HOW TO SPOT

**Size:** 6 to 12 inches (15.2 to 30.5 cm) tall
**Flower:** White spathe around a spadix, 4 to 5 inches (10.2 to 12.7 cm) tall
**Habitat:** Wetlands
**Range:** Northern Canada and the northern United States

# WESTERN SKUNK CABBAGE

## *(LYSICHITON AMERICANUS)*

When it blooms, the western skunk cabbage produces a bad-smelling odor that attracts insects to help ensure pollination. Its flowers feature a bright yellow spathe surrounding an upright spadix covered in tiny flowers. The western skunk cabbage has large leaves, which are waxy, tall, and wide and grow upright from the short stalk. Skunk cabbage is toxic if handled or ingested. It can cause burning of the mouth and difficulty swallowing.

### HOW TO SPOT

**Size:** 12 to 60 in (30.5 cm to 1.5 m) tall

**Flower:** Bright yellow spathe around a spadix, 3 to 5 inches (7.6 to 12.7 cm) tall

**Habitat:** Wetlands and woodlands

**Range:** Western Canada and the northwestern and central United States

# FLAME AZALEA

## *(RHODODENDRON CALENDULACEUM)*

The flame azalea gets its common name from its bright funnel-shaped flowers, which can be vibrant orange or fiery red, with buds that resemble candle flames. Its blooms are larger than most other North American azaleas. The stamens, or male fertilizing organs, are also distinctive. They stick out almost three times as far as the rest of the flower. If ingested, all parts of the flame azalea are poisonous and considered particularly dangerous to dogs, cats, and horses.

### HOW TO SPOT

**Size:** 4 to 8 feet (1.2 to 2.4 m) tall

**Flower:** Bright orange or red, very long stamens, 3 inches (7.6 cm) in diameter

**Habitat:** Woodland slopes and grasslands at high elevations

**Range:** Eastern United States

### WHAT ARE AZALEAS?

Azaleas are flowering shrubs that produce large quantities of bright flowers. They grow abundantly throughout Canada and the United States, especially in the Southeast. Azaleas are also very toxic plants, especially in their leaves and nectar. Ingesting these can affect the digestive and nervous systems and cause vomiting, seizures, and potentially organ failure.

# MOUNTAIN AZALEA

## *(RHODODENDRON CANESCENS)*

The mountain azalea has clusters of small, funnel-shaped flowers with five petals each. The stamens extend well beyond the rest of the bloom. The flowers of mountain azaleas are usually pale pink and small. Mountain azaleas grow in swampy areas and often form colonies, or clusters of many plants. All parts of the mountain azalea are highly toxic to humans and animals. They can be fatal if eaten. Ingesting the plant can cause digestive distress, paralysis, and coma.

### HOW TO SPOT

**Size:** 6 to 15 feet (1.8 to 4.6 m) tall

**Flower:** Pale pink, 1 to 3 inches (2.5 to 7.6 cm) long

**Habitat:** Swampy areas and wet woodlands

**Range:** Southeastern United States

# PLUMLEAF AZALEA

## *(RHODODENDRON PRUNIFOLIUM)*

The plumleaf azalea is the rarest in the wild. Plumleaf azaleas grow larger than most other azaleas. Unlike other species, though, they have broad leaves that are not hairy. Their funnel-shaped flowers are small and orange-red to dark red. The flowers bloom in clusters and have long stamens that stick out well beyond the petals. Plumleaf azaleas are toxic to humans and animals and can cause vomiting, diarrhea, paralysis, and coma if ingested.

### FUN FACT

**The plumleaf azalea's small native range is unfortunately shrinking due to logging and development.**

### HOW TO SPOT

**Size:** 8 to 12 feet (2.4 to 3.7 m) tall
**Flower:** Red, up to 3 inches (7.6 cm) in diameter
**Habitat:** Moist ravines along the Chattahoochee River
**Range:** Alabama and Georgia

# SWEET AZALEA

## *(RHODODENDRON ARBORESCENS)*

The sweet azalea has glossy, hairless leaves. Small, white, funnel-shaped flowers bloom later in the spring than those of other azaleas. They appear in clusters and have distinctive long, red stamens. They are also considered more fragrant, or stronger smelling, than other azaleas. Likewise, sweet azalea leaves are unusual because they are green on top but white on the underside. All parts of the sweet azalea are highly toxic, and ingesting large quantities could be fatal.

### HOW TO SPOT

**Size:** 8 to 20 feet (2.4 to 6.1 m) tall

**Flower:** White with long red stamens, up to 3 inches (7.6 cm) in diameter

**Habitat:** Wet mountainous areas and along streams

**Range:** Eastern United States

# RED BANEBERRY *(ACTAEA RUBRA)*

Especially common in the Pacific Northwest, red baneberry bushes have leaves in clusters of three on long stalks. These leaves have deep teeth along their edges and hairy veins on their undersides. Red baneberry flowers have white petals, multiple stamens, and a feathery look. Bright red, oval, waxy berries have a black spot at the center. Red baneberries are extremely poisonous and can be fatal if eaten. They affect the digestive system and heart.

## HOW TO SPOT

**Size:** 1 to 2 feet (0.3 to 0.6 m) tall
**Fruit:** Red berries with a black spot, 0.3 inches (0.8 cm) long
**Habitat:** Shady woodlands
**Range:** Canada and the northern United States

### FUN FACT

Baneberries are harmless to birds, who eat them and scatter their seeds.

## WHAT ARE BANEBERRIES?

The baneberry plant is a shrub characterized by its berries, long root system, and large, tooth-edged leaves with hairy undersides. Red and white baneberry shrubs are highly poisonous, and eating just a few berries can cause dangerous symptoms, including mouth burns, digestive upset, respiratory problems, and cardiac arrest.

# WHITE BANEBERRY

## *(ACTAEA PACHYPODA)*

White and red baneberries are often found near each other. White baneberry shrubs have larger stems and grow taller and wider than red baneberries. But the main difference is the color of their berries. White baneberry shrubs produce oval, white berries with noticeable black spots, with stems that turn bright pink or red as they mature. White baneberries are highly poisonous and can affect the heart muscle and cause cardiac arrest in humans.

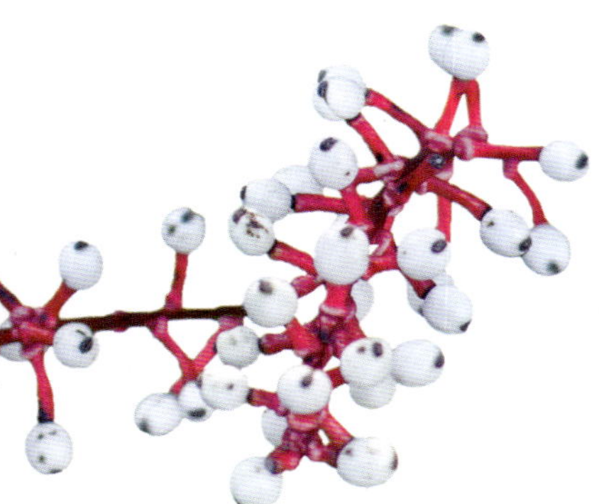

### HOW TO SPOT

**Size:** 2 to 3 feet (0.6 to 0.9 m) tall; 2 to 3 feet (0.6 to 0.9 m) wide

**Fruit:** White berries with a black spot, 0.3 inches (0.8 cm) long

**Habitat:** Shady woodlands

**Range:** Eastern Canada and the midwestern and eastern United States

# BIG BEND BLUEBONNET

## *(LUPINUS HAVARDII)*

Big Bend bluebonnets are taller than other bluebonnet species. Their thick, upright, branching stems support narrow clusters of flowers. Typically, these flowers are a deep blue color with a large yellow patch in the center. Flowers bloom on the upper part of the plant's stem, above narrow, palm-shaped leaves that grow close to the ground. Big Bend bluebonnets are toxic, especially in their seeds, and can cause respiratory problems.

### HOW TO SPOT

**Size:** Up to 3 or 4 feet (0.9 to 1.2 m) tall

**Flower:** Dark blue with yellow patch, 0.7 inches (1.8 cm) long

**Habitat:** Deserts, rocky terrain, and mountain slopes

**Range:** Southwestern United States, especially Texas, and northwestern Mexico

### WHAT ARE BLUEBONNETS?

Widespread throughout North America, bluebonnets are small blue or purple wildflowers that can fill large areas of open land. Bluebonnets are part of the pea family, and their flowers are shaped like pea flowers. They attract bees, hummingbirds, and butterflies but are toxic to humans, pets, and grazing animals such as cattle, horses, and sheep.

# SILVERY LUPINE *(LUPINUS ARGENTEUS)*

Like most bluebonnets, silvery lupine bluebonnets have tall, hairy, spiky stalks. These stalks are surrounded by clusters of flowers. Their stalks and leaves are a silvery color. Their flowers are much lighter in color than those of other common bluebells. Flowers are light blue or violet. Silvery lupines are poisonous in their seeds and leaves. Ingesting silvery lupine can cause vomiting, diarrhea, and dizziness.

## HOW TO SPOT

**Size:** 1 to 2 feet (0.3 to 0.6 m) tall

**Flower:** Light blue, 0.2 to 0.6 inches (0.5 to 1.5 cm) long

**Habitat:** Deserts, grasslands, forests, and rocky terrain

**Range:** Southwestern Canada through the southwest United States

# TEXAS BLUEBONNET

## *(LUPINUS TEXENSIS)*

Fields of Texas bluebonnets are a common sight along the roadways of Texas from late March to early May. They have larger leaves with sharper points than other species. They also produce more numerous flower clusters, up to 50 flowers per plant. Texas bluebonnet flowers are fragrant and a bright, deep, purple-blue color. They also have a distinctive white color on the top of their flower spikes. Ingesting this plant can damage the nervous system.

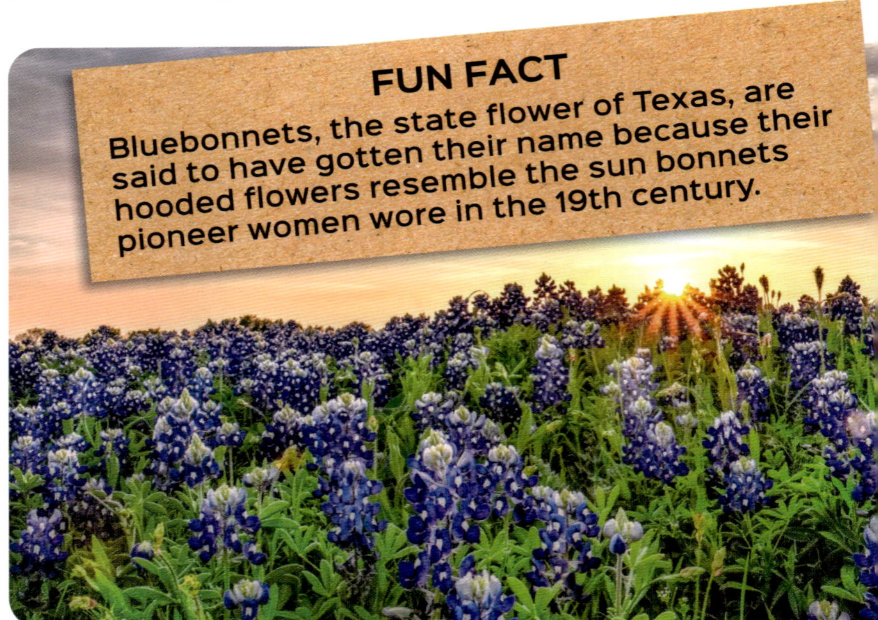

**FUN FACT**

**Bluebonnets, the state flower of Texas, are said to have gotten their name because their hooded flowers resemble the sun bonnets pioneer women wore in the 19th century.**

## HOW TO SPOT

**Size:** 1 to 2 feet (0.3 to 0.6 m) tall

**Flower:** Bright blue with white tips, 0.4 to 0.8 inches (1 to 2 cm) long

**Habitat:** Open fields, prairies, roadsides, and disturbed areas

**Range:** Southwestern and southeastern United States and northern Mexico

# WILD LUPINE *(LUPINUS PERENNIS)*

The flowers of the wild lupine are usually a light or whitish blue or purple. Its flower clusters are more widely spaced than those of other species. Wild lupine has become endangered in some areas. Wild lupine is the main source of food for the Karner blue butterfly caterpillar. So this species has also become endangered. Wild lupine is poisonous and can cause dizziness, confusion, and respiratory problems when ingested.

## HOW TO SPOT

**Size:** 2 inches (5.1 cm) tall

**Flower:** Whitish blue or light purple, 0.8 to 1 inch (2 to 2.5 cm) long

**Habitat:** Sandy areas, hills, and open woods

**Range:** Eastern North America, from Nova Scotia to Florida

# NORTHERN WOLFSBANE

## *(ACONITUM LYCOCTONUM)*

The northern wolfsbane plant has a tall, upright stem. The palm-shaped leaves have deep, toothy lobes at their base. Its flowers are narrowly spaced around a thin stem, above the leaves. They range from dark purple-blue to lavender and can also be pale yellow. Northern wolfsbane flowers have a distinctive hooded shape. They are highly poisonous. They cause disruption in the connection between nerves and muscles when ingested.

### HOW TO SPOT

**Size:** Up to 3.3 feet (1 m) tall

**Flower:** Violet with a hooded shape, 0.7 to 1 inch (1.8 to 2.5 cm) long

**Habitat:** Shady woodlands with moist soils

**Range:** Eastern Canada

### FUN FACT

Wolfsbane got its common name because it was historically used to kill wolves, while monkshood was thought to resemble the hoods worn by medieval monks.

# WESTERN MONKSHOOD

## *(ACONITUM COLUMBIANUM)*

The western monkshood has palm-shaped leaves with deep, pointed lobes. Its thin, spindle-shaped stem has widely spaced flowers that are usually blue or purple but can sometimes be white. These flowers usually have spurs. Their top petals have upright folds that form a distinctive hooded shape. All parts of western monkshood are extremely poisonous and can cause death. Ingestion hurts the heart and lungs.

### HOW TO SPOT

**Size:** 2 to 6 feet (0.6 to 1.8 m) tall
**Flower:** Blue with a hooded shape, 0.7 to 2.2 inches (1.8 to 5.6 cm) long
**Habitat:** Meadows and coniferous forests with moist soils
**Range:** Western North America

### WHAT ARE BUTTERCUPS?

Buttercups are a large family of more than 2,000 different flowering plants. Most of these species produce brightly colored flowers. One genus of the buttercup family is called *Aconitum*. The *Aconitum* genus includes more than 250 species, and most of these are extremely poisonous.

# PEYOTE CACTUS

## *(LOPHOPHORA WILLIAMSII)*

The peyote cactus does not have spines. It has a rounded body that grows close to the ground. It has a distinctive bluish-green color. This cactus grows in small clusters that look like buttons or pincushions topped with small tufts called areoles. During the day, the peyote cactus blooms with wide pink or white flowers on the top of its rounded stem. Ingesting it can cause hallucinations, vomiting, dizziness, difficulty breathing, and increased blood pressure and heart rate.

### FUN FACT

Peyote has cultural significance because American Indian peoples have used it for medicine and rituals for more than 5,500 years.

### HOW TO SPOT

**Size:** 2 inches (5.1 cm) tall; up to 4 inches (10.2 cm) in diameter

**Flower:** Pink or white, 0.4 to 0.9 inches (1 to 2.3 cm) in diameter

**Habitat:** Dry desert areas

**Range:** Southwestern United States and Mexico

# TEDDY BEAR CACTUS

## *(CYLINDROPUNTIA BIGELOVII)*

The teddy bear, or cholla, cactus stands upright, with a thick trunk that branches at the top. Small yellow-green flowers bloom at the tops of its stems. The teddy bear cactus gets its common name because its stems are completely covered in small spines, giving it a fuzzy look. However, these needles are very sharp and painful to remove when they stick in the skin. These spikes are also the most dangerous part of the plant. Although they are not poisonous, they can cause skin irritation, injury, and infection.

### HOW TO SPOT

**Size:** 1 to 5 feet (0.3 to 1.5 m) tall

**Flower:** Yellow-green, 1.4 inches (3.6 cm) long

**Habitat:** Desert areas with high elevations

**Range:** Southwestern United States and northwest Mexico

### WHAT ARE CACTI?

Cactuses or cacti thrive in dry, desert areas where most other plants cannot grow. They are able to take water from the soil and store it inside their thick, fleshy, tough-skinned stems. Many cactus plants have sharp needles or spines around their stems, and they typically have no leaves.

# POISON HEMLOCK *(CONIUM MACULATUM)*

Poison hemlock is one of the deadliest plants in North America. All parts of the plant are poisonous if handled, inhaled, or ingested. If eaten, it can be fatal, causing severe vomiting, seizures, respiratory failure, paralysis, and coma. Poison hemlock plants often have an unpleasant smell. Their leaves are concentrated around the base of the plant, with large veins on the underside. Tiny white flowers form umbrella-shaped clusters. The stem is hollow with very distinctive dark, purplish spots.

## HOW TO SPOT

**Size:** 6 to 10 feet (1.8 to 3 m) tall
**Stem:** Thick and hollow; hairless with purplish spots
**Flower:** White, in umbrella-shaped clusters 3 inches (7.6 cm) in diameter
**Habitat:** Stream banks, ditches, fields, and disturbed areas
**Range:** Throughout North America

## WHAT IS THE CARROT FAMILY?

The carrot family includes more than 3,700 species. The plants have taproots, or long, thick, underground roots shaped like carrots. Most of these species also have flower clusters shaped like umbrellas at the top of the stem. Some species of the carrot family, such as carrots and parsnips, are edible. Others can be extremely poisonous when touched or ingested.

# WILD PARSNIP *(PASTINACA SATIVA)*

Wild parsnip flowers appear in wide, umbrella-shaped flowerheads on long, thin stems. These clusters are made up of tiny yellow flowers with five petals each. The leaves of wild parsnip plants have very deep teeth and are concentrated mainly around the plant's base. The sap of the wild parsnip makes skin extremely sensitive to sunlight, causing severe rashes and blisters.

## HOW TO SPOT

**Size:** 2 to 6 feet (0.6 to 1.8 m) tall

**Flower:** Yellow, in umbrella-shaped clusters 4 to 8 inches (10.2 to 20.3 cm) in diameter

**Habitat:** Sunny prairies, roadsides, and pastures

**Range:** Throughout Canada and the United States

# AMERICAN BLACK ELDERBERRY

## *(SAMBUCUS CANADENSIS)*

The American black elderberry is a shrub with feathery leaves and dark berries. Its leaves have fine teeth and grow on each side of a central stem in opposite pairs. American black elderberry blooms in broad clusters of tiny white flowers. In the fall, they form hanging clusters of dark purple or black berries. Unripe or raw berries, as well as the stem, root, seeds, and leaves, are toxic. They can cause vomiting, stomach cramps and digestive upset, and dizziness.

### HOW TO SPOT

**Size:** 6.5 to 13 feet (2 to 4 m) tall

**Fruit:** Purple to black berries, 0.25 inches (0.6 cm) in diameter

**Habitat:** Wetlands, riverbanks, moist meadows, and forest edges

**Range:** Eastern to central Canada and the northern, eastern, and southeastern United States

### WHAT ARE ELDERBERRIES?

Elderberry or elderflower plants have flowerheads that may contain hundreds of very small, white flowers growing in clusters. The shrubs also produce small berries, which range from dark purple or black to blue or red.

# RED ELDERBERRY

## *(SAMBUCUS RACEMOSA)*

This shrub has long, oval-shaped leaves with pointed ends and irregular teeth. These leaves have a strong odor when crushed. Flattened flowerheads form from clusters of hundreds of tiny white flowers. Red elderberry also produces bright red berries that grow in pyramid-shaped clusters and do not droop. These berries are very toxic when raw or unripe, and the stem, roots, and leaves are also poisonous. Ingesting them can cause vomiting, diarrhea, and difficulty breathing.

### HOW TO SPOT

**Size:** 8 to 12 feet (2.4 to 3.7 m) tall

**Fruit:** Red berries, 0.25 inches (0.6 cm) in diameter

**Habitat:** Wetlands, moist meadows, old growth forests, and near rivers and streams

**Range:** Across Canada and the north and central United States

# CALLA LILY *(ZANTEDESCHIA AETHIOPICA)*

The blooms of calla lilies have a bright white spathe wrapped around an upright yellow spadix. The flowers give off a light fragrance. Calla lilies thrive in shallow water and swampy areas. They are especially common from Louisiana to Florida. The leaves of calla lilies grow in clumps. They are dark green and wide, with an arrow or heart shape. The stems and leaves are the most poisonous parts of the plant, and they can burn the mouth, tongue, and throat and cause abdominal pain and diarrhea.

## HOW TO SPOT

**Size:** 2 to 3 feet (0.6 to 0.9 cm) tall
**Flower:** White spathe up to 10 inches (25.4 cm) long around a yellow spadix
**Habitat:** Wetlands, streams and ponds
**Range:** US Atlantic and Gulf Coasts

## WHAT ARE FALSE LILIES?

False lily is a common name for different types of flowering plants that resemble true lilies but are not part of the Lilium family. The term *false lily* applies to numerous species that come in different shapes and sizes and may grow in distinct habitats and ranges.

# DAYLILY *(HEMEROCALLIS FULVA)*

Because they do not grow from bulbs, daylilies are not considered true lilies. Daylily flowers are trumpet-shaped. They are usually brightly colored with six stamens. The plants grow in clumps and have long, blade-like leaves. They also have white areas between the stem and leaves. The most center part of the flower is generally a different color from the rest of the petals. Daylilies contain toxic compounds that can cause digestive issues. They are especially harmful to cats.

## HOW TO SPOT

**Size:** 1 to 4 feet (0.3 to 1.2 m) tall
**Flower:** Brightly colored, 3 to 6 inches (7.6 to 15.2 cm) in diameter
**Habitat:** Woodlands, grassy meadows and fields, and wetlands
**Range:** Throughout North America

# LILY OF THE VALLEY

## *(CONVALLARIA MAJALIS)*

Lily of the valley tends to form colonies. It can spread very aggressively. Its leaves grow at the base of the plant, and the flowers bloom along a tall, thin stem. The flowers are white and pendent, or hanging. They have a distinctive bell shape. All parts of the plant are very poisonous, including the bright red berries that appear after the flowers bloom. Even small amounts can cause rashes, stomach pain, blurred vision, vomiting, and reduced heart rate.

**FUN FACT**

**Although the plant is highly toxic, lily of the valley is often used in perfume because of its pleasant fresh scent.**

## HOW TO SPOT

**Size:** 6 to 12 inches (15.2 to 30.5 cm) tall
**Flower:** White, 0.2 to 0.4 inches (0.5 to 1 cm) in diameter
**Habitat:** Woodlands
**Range:** East, central, and northwest North America

# PEACE LILY *(SPATHIPHYLLUM WALLISII)*

The peace lily has full, abundant, dark green leaves that are glossy, long, and pointed. They grow from the base of the plant. Peace lily flowers have a white spathe that partially surrounds a spiky, yellowish-green spadix. Each plant produces one or two flowers in spring. In the wild, peace lilies thrive in the warm, moist soils of the forest. All parts of the plant are toxic, and ingestion can cause mouth irritation, difficulty swallowing, and diarrhea.

## HOW TO SPOT

**Size:** 12 to 15 inches (30.5 to 38.1 cm) tall
**Leaves:** Up to 1.5 feet (0.5 m) long; 6 inches (15.2 cm) wide
**Habitat:** Shady and moist forest floors
**Range:** Southeastern United States and Mexico

# BLACK HELLEBORE

## *(HELLEBORUS NIGER)*

Despite its name, black hellebore flowers are not black, but white with a pink tinge. They are cup-shaped with overlapping petals and a crown of many yellow stamens in the center. The leaves of the black hellebore are glossy, leathery, and shaped like pointed arrows. They are usually hairless with toothy edges. All parts of the plant are poisonous to humans when handled or ingested, causing symptoms ranging from skin rashes to vomiting and slowing of the heart.

### HOW TO SPOT

**Size:** 6 to 12 inches (15.2 to 30.5 cm) tall

**Flower:** White, 3.8 inches (9.7 cm) in diameter

**Habitat:** Mountainous terrain in colder regions

**Range:** Canada and across the northern United States

### WHAT ARE HELLEBORES?

Hellebores are small flowering plants that are part of the buttercup family. Hellebores thrive in cold climates and often bloom in the winter.

# LENTEN ROSE *(HELLEBORUS ORIENTALIS)*

Like other hellebores, the Lenten rose thrives in cold climates. Its leaves are leathery and coarse, with deep teeth at the edges. The Lenten rose has flowers that are large, cup-shaped, and drooping. They can be white, pink, or deep purple with spots, and they have a prominent center crown with many yellow stamens. All parts of this plant are poisonous to humans. Its sap can cause skin irritation, and ingesting the plant can cause vomiting and diarrhea.

**FUN FACT**

**The common name "Lenten rose" developed because this species blooms around the period of Lent celebrated by many Christians.**

## HOW TO SPOT

**Size:** 1 to 1.5 feet (0.3 to 0.5 m) tall
**Flower:** White or pink, 1 to 3 inches (2.5 to 7.6 cm) in diameter
**Habitat:** Forest edges and meadows in northern climates
**Range:** Canada and across the northern United States

# CADE JUNIPER *(JUNIPERUS OXYCEDRUS)*

The cade juniper can be a shrub or small tree. It has distinctive red bark and stiff, needle-like leaves that grow in whorls of three around the stem. These needles can be prickly, and they have distinct white veins down the center. Cade junipers make cones that look like waxy green berries that become red or orange as they ripen. Cade junipers produce tar called cade oil, which can be toxic. It affects the liver, heart, skin, respiratory tract, and nervous systems.

## HOW TO SPOT

**Size:** Up to 49 feet (14.9 m) tall

**Fruit:** Round, red, berry-like cones, 0.3 to 0.5 inches (0.8 to 1.3 cm) in diameter

**Habitat:** Dry, sandy hills and rocky terrain

**Range:** Eastern United States

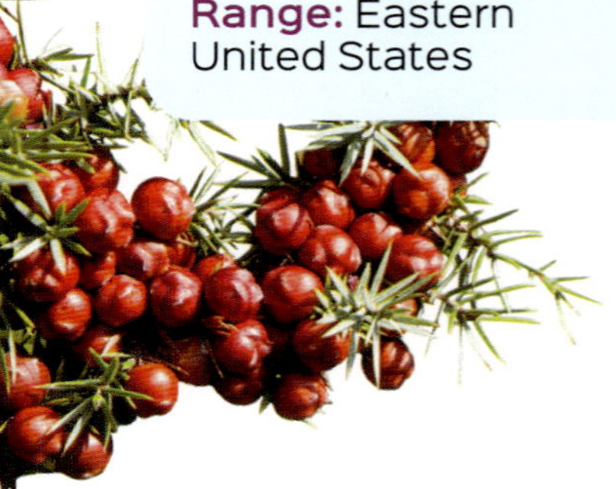

## WHAT ARE JUNIPERS?

Junipers are trees and shrubs in the cypress family. Junipers are evergreen, meaning that they keep their leaves year-round and do not lose them in winter. Instead of flat leaves, junipers have needles, and they are coniferous. This means they produce cones with seeds inside. However, these cones look more like berries, and they are usually blue or red.

# SAVIN JUNIPER *(JUNIPERUS SABINA)*

The savin juniper is a spreading shrub. It often grows low to the ground. Young plants have needle-like leaves but may develop scaly, feathery leaves as they mature. The savin juniper produces cones that contain one to three seeds. These cones are round and fleshy. They look like blue berries with a white, waxy coating. All parts of the savin juniper are poisonous, especially its savin oil, which can affect the digestive and nervous system and damage the kidneys.

## HOW TO SPOT

**Size:** 4 to 6 feet (1.2 to 1.8 m) tall with a variable shape

**Fruit:** Round, blue, berry-like cones, 0.2 to 0.4 inches (0.5 to 1 cm) in diameter

**Habitat:** Rocky or mountainous terrain in high elevations

**Range:** Canada and eastern and central United States

# CARDINAL LARKSPUR

## *(DELPHINIUM CARDINALE)*

Cardinal larkspur has bright red flowers that grow widely spaced along a thin, upright stem. They have curling edges and bright yellow blotches on the top two petals. The flowers also have a long spur at the back and stick far out from the stem. Its leaves are wide and palm-shaped, with many deep lobes. This species can cause skin rashes when handled and digestive problems when ingested. Due to their grazing, cattle are the most often affected.

### HOW TO SPOT

**Size:** Up to 6 feet (1.8 m) tall
**Flower:** Red, with a long spur, up to 3 inches (7.6 cm) in diameter
**Habitat:** Dry slopes with sandy or rocky soil
**Range:** Southern California and Baja California

### FUN FACT

Larkspur species that grow in mountainous regions are much taller than those that grow in prairies.

### WHAT ARE LARKSPURS?

Larkspurs are flowering plants. They have tall, upright stems and blue, purple, or red flowers characterized by long, narrow spurs at the back. The flowers stick far out from the stem on long stalks. All parts of larkspurs are poisonous.

# CAROLINA LARKSPUR

## *(DELPHINIUM CAROLINIANUM)*

The Carolina larkspur has a thin, hairy stem. The widely spaced, cup-shaped flowers are smaller than those of other larkspurs. These flowers project out on long stalks. They have long spurs in the back. They are usually blue or purple with a dark spot on each petal. The leaves are wide and palm-shaped, with deep lobes. All parts of the plant are poisonous. They can cause heart failure and lung paralysis that can be fatal, especially in animals.

### HOW TO SPOT

**Size:** 1 to 3 feet (0.3 to 0.9 m) tall

**Flower:** Blue or purple, with a long spur, up to 1 inch (2.5 cm) wide

**Habitat:** Prairies and rocky terrain

**Range:** Central, eastern, and southeastern United States

### FUN FACT

Bees have evolved to see blue and purple colors well, so they are very attracted to Carolina larkspurs.

# SIERRA LARKSPUR

## *(DELPHINIUM GLAUCUM)*

The Sierra larkspur, or mountain larkspur, is a tall plant with lobed, palm-shaped leaves at the base. Each upright stem is surrounded by more than 50 widely spaced flowers. Sierra larkspur flowers have long, slender spurs at the back and stick out from the stem at almost 90-degree angles. The flowers are mostly a dark blue or deep purple, with white petals at the top. Sometimes its petals look wrinkly. Sierra larkspurs are toxic and can kill grazing cattle.

### HOW TO SPOT

**Size:** 5 to 9 feet (1.5 to 2.7 m) tall

**Flower:** Blue or purple, with a long spur, 0.7 to 1.1 inches (1.8 to 2.8 cm) in diameter

**Habitat:** Mountainous areas, riverbanks, and meadows at high altitudes

**Range:** Western North America

# TWO-LOBE LARKSPUR

## *(DELPHINIUM NUTTALLIANUM)*

The two-lobe larkspur is small, with an upright stem that may be white, green, or pink. Its palm-shaped leaves have deep lobes and are located only at the base of the plant. Its flowers are widely spaced around the stem. They range in color from light blue to purple, with white upper petals and a long, narrow spur at the back. Each plant may produce up to a dozen blooms. Two-lobe larkspurs can cause vomiting, muscle weakness, paralysis, and irregular heart beat when ingested.

### HOW TO SPOT

**Size:** 1.6 feet (0.5 m) tall

**Flower:** Blue or purple, with a very long spur, 0.7 to 1 inch (1.8 to 2.5 cm) in diameter

**Habitat:** Forests, meadows and along streams

**Range:** Western Canada and western and central United States

# EASTER LILY *(LILIUM LONGIFLORUM)*

The Easter lily is also called the trumpet lily. It has long, oval-shaped leaves with a horizontal vein. The flowers are trumpet-shaped and bloom at the top of a long, sturdy, rigid stalk. These flowers are bright white and very large, with six petals around groups of stamen in the center. They are very fragrant and do not wither for up to two weeks. Easter lilies are known to be especially dangerous for cats, and even licking pollen from their fur can cause dangerous illness.

## HOW TO SPOT

**Size:** 2 to 3 feet (0.6 to 0.9 m) tall

**Flower:** White, 5 inches (12.7 cm) in diameter

**Habitat:** Coastal areas

**Range:** Pacific Northwest, southeastern United States

## WHAT ARE LILIES?

Lilies are flowering plants with narrow leaves and wide stems that produce large, bright, trumpet-shaped flowers with a strong fragrance. Lilies are toxic to humans and animals, especially cats. All true lilies grow from bulbs under the soil. Bulbs are the ball-like part of the plant that stores food.

## ORIENTAL LILY *(LILIUM ORIENTALIS)*

The oriental lily is taller than other species of lily and produces larger flowers. The flowers are trumpet-shaped and very fragrant, with six petals each. They bloom in a variety of very bright colors, such as orange, red, and deep pink. They may be open and outward-facing or hanging. The plant has oval-shaped leaves that are very long, with a horizontal vein. The entire plant is toxic. It can cause burning, vomiting, and diarrhea when ingested.

### HOW TO SPOT

**Size:** 3 to 6 feet (0.9 to 1.8 m) tall
**Flower:** Bright-colored, up to 10 inches (25.4 cm) in diameter
**Habitat:** Woodlands, grasslands, and marshlands
**Range:** Southern Canada, across the United States, and northern Mexico

# TIGER LILY

## *(LILIUM LANCIFOLIUM OR LILIUM TIGRINUM)*

The tiger lily gets its common name because its orange flowers have dark spots near the base of their petals, resembling a tiger's coat. Its flowers face downward and their petals curve slightly backward. This makes their numerous center stamen look more prominent. Tiger lilies have long, pointed leaves with a horizontal vein. Tiger lilies are very toxic to cats and dogs. They cause digestive distress when ingested.

### HOW TO SPOT

**Size:** 2 to 5 feet (0.6 to 1.5 m) tall
**Flower:** Spotted orange, 5 inches (12.7 cm) in diameter
**Habitat:** Coastal or woodland areas
**Range:** Eastern and southeastern United States, especially Georgia

# TURK'S CAP LILY *(LILIUM SUPERBUM)*

The Turk's cap lily is the tallest lily in North America. Its flowers point downward, with heavily spotted orange petals that curve back to the base. Their flowers are green in the center, and their stamens have very long antlers with orange tips. Turk's cap lilies have whorled leaves, or three leaves that grow from a single point and wrap around the stem. Ingesting any part of the Turk's cap lily can be dangerous to cats, causing vomiting and digestive problems.

## HOW TO SPOT

**Size:** 4 to 6 feet (1.2 to 1.8 m) tall

**Flower:** Spotted orange, up to 8 inches (20.3 cm) in diameter

**Habitat:** Wet woodlands, forest meadows, and forest edges

**Range:** Eastern and southeastern United States

### FUN FACT

Turk's cap lilies and tiger lilies can produce up to 40 blossoms from one bulb, more than double the number that most species make.

# AMERICAN BLACK NIGHTSHADE

## *(SOLANUM AMERICANUM)*

The American black nightshade grows in a wide variety of habitats. Its leaves have coarse, wavy edges. Its flowers are small, white, and star-shaped. Its fruits start out green and then ripen into shiny, black, slightly egg-shaped berries. All parts of the plant, and especially the leaves and berries, are extremely poisonous and potentially fatal if ingested. They affect the heart, lungs, nervous system, and digestive system.

### HOW TO SPOT

**Size:** 3.3 to 5 feet (1 to 1.5 m) tall

**Fruit:** Black, less than 0.25 inches (0.6 cm) in diameter

**Habitat:** Forests, grasslands, mountain slopes, and fields

**Range:** Throughout North America

### WHAT ARE NIGHTSHADES?

Nightshades are a group of flowering plants that often have poisonous leaves and berries. The berries are usually either black or red when mature. Certain species of nightshade can cause convulsions and death if ingested.

# BITTERSWEET NIGHTSHADE

## *(SOLANUM DULCAMARA)*

Bittersweet nightshade is a low-climbing vine. It has many branches that can sprawl along the ground or wrap around trees and shrubs. The plant produces lobed leaves with smooth edges. The small, star-shaped flowers have purple petals that curve backward. Its mature oval berries are red. All parts of the plant are highly poisonous and potentially fatal to humans and livestock. It causes vomiting, diarrhea, convulsions, slowed breathing, and even death.

### HOW TO SPOT

**Size:** 3.3 to 10 feet (1 to 3 m) tall

**Fruit:** Red, 0.4 to 0.5 inches (1 to 1.3 cm) in diameter

**Habitat:** Wetlands, woodlands, marshes, and scrubland

**Range:** Western and central Canada, across the United States

# DEADLY NIGHTSHADE

## *(ATROPA BELLADONNA)*

Deadly nightshade is a shrub or weed. It has tall branches and long, oval-shaped leaves with smooth edges. Its flowers are small and bell-shaped, with dull purple petals that are green at the base. After the flowers die, green, oval berries appear and ripen to black. These berries and all other parts of the plant are extremely poisonous. They can affect the heart and cause convulsions, hallucinations, and death. Ingesting even a few berries can kill a child or an adult.

### HOW TO SPOT

**Size:** 3 to 5 feet (0.9 to 1.5 m) tall
**Fruit:** Black, 0.6 to 0.8 inches (1.5 to 2 cm) in diameter
**Habitat:** Woodlands, wastelands, roadsides, disturbed areas
**Range:** New York, Washington, Oregon, California, and Michigan

# JERUSALEM CHERRY

## *(SOLANUM PSEUDOCAPSICUM)*

The Jerusalem cherry is a small, upright, bushy shrub. It grows in many different habitats. It has long, narrow, arrow-shaped leaves with wavy edges. The shrub produces small, white, star-shaped flowers. Its berries can be red, yellow, or orange and look very similar to cherry tomatoes. All parts of the plant are toxic, especially the berries. Handling it can cause skin irritation. Ingesting it can cause stomach upset, respiratory problems, seizures, shock, and sometimes even death.

### HOW TO SPOT

**Size:** 0.8 to 3 feet (0.2 to 0.9 m) tall
**Fruit:** Red, yellow or orange, up to 0.6 inches (1.5 cm) in diameter
**Habitat:** Coastal and subtropical and tropical areas
**Range:** Eastern and southeastern United States, southwestern Mexico

# JIMSON WEED *(DATURA STRAMONIUM)*

Jimson weed has stout stems that may be reddish or purple. They fork off into branches, each with a single fragrant flower that opens at night. The flowers are funnel-shaped and either white or lavender. Its leaves are long and smooth but have teeth at their edges. The stem and leaves may have an unpleasant odor. All parts of the jimson weed are poisonous. It can cause vomiting, seizures, hallucinations, and coma.

## HOW TO SPOT

**Size:** 2 to 5 feet (0.6 to 1.5 m) tall
**Flower:** White to light purple, 3 inches (7.6 cm) in diameter
**Habitat:** Pastures, open fields, and disturbed lands
**Range:** Throughout North America

### FUN FACT

Because their flowers open at night, jimson weed and sacred datura thornapple attract moths.

# SACRED DATURA THORNAPPLE

## *(DATURA WRIGHTII)*

The sacred datura thornapple is a sprawling, upright shrub or trailing vine with dense leaves. Its leaves are oval with fine hairs and wavy edges. They have rounded bases but pointy tips. The flowers are long, white, and trumpet-shaped, sometimes with a purple tinge. Five distinctive points appear spaced symmetrically around the flower petals. The flowers have a sweet fragrance and open at night. Sacred datura thornapples are highly toxic when ingested.

### HOW TO SPOT

**Size:** 4 to 5 feet (1.2 to 1.5 m) tall

**Flower:** White, 1.5 to 5 inches (3.8 to 12.7 cm) in diameter

**Habitat:** Pastures, open fields, and disturbed lands

**Range:** Southwestern United States and northwestern Mexico

# WHITE OLEANDER *(NERIUM OLEANDER)*

White oleander is a large, upright shrub. It has many waxy, fan-like leaves that grow in whorls of three. Funnel-shaped oleander flowers have five petals and are often fragrant. They appear in abundant clusters and bloom in many colors, including pink, white, and red. All parts of the oleander plant are highly toxic. Its sap can irritate the skin. Ingesting the plant can affect the heart, digestive system, and nervous system. It can sometimes be fatal to humans, pets, and livestock.

## HOW TO SPOT

**Size:** 4 to 20 feet (1.2 to 6 m) tall
**Flower:** White or pink, 1 to 2 inches (2.5 to 5.1 cm) in diameter
**Habitat:** Coastal areas and near streams
**Range:** Southeastern and southwestern United States and Mexico

## WHAT IS OLEANDER?

Oleander is an upright, bushy shrub that can grow very large. It can withstand difficult growing conditions, such as pollution or drought. It thrives in areas that have been damaged or changed by human activity.

# YELLOW OLEANDER

## *(CASCABELA THEVETIA)*

The yellow oleander plant grows in more tropical regions and can be larger in its native habitat than white oleander. Instead of whorled leaves, it has waxy, blade-like leaves that grow out from each side of the stem. Its flowers are bright yellow rather than white or pink. They are funnel-shaped with five petals. All parts of the yellow oleander plant are highly poisonous and potentially fatal to humans and animals. They cause vomiting and diarrhea.

### HOW TO SPOT

**Size:** 10 to 30 feet (3 to 9.1 m) tall; 6.5 to 16 feet (2 to 4.9 m) wide
**Flower:** Yellow, 1 to 3 inches (2.5 to 7.6 cm) in diameter
**Habitat:** Tropical coastal areas and near streams
**Range:** Mexico

# AUTUMN CROCUS

## *(COLCHICUM AUTUMNALE)*

The autumn crocus blooms in the fall. They produce flowers in a variety of colors. The star-shaped flower has six stamens. These blooms emerge from the ground before the long, narrow, arrow-shaped leaves. All parts of the plant are very poisonous. Ingestion can cause vomiting, diarrhea, organ failure, and ultimately death.

### HOW TO SPOT

**Size:** 0.5 to 1 foot (0.2 to 0.3 m) tall
**Flower:** Purple, pink, white or yellow, 2 to 3 inches (5.1 to 7.6 cm) in diameter
**Habitat:** Woodlands and damp meadows
**Range:** Western and central Canada and the eastern and midwestern United States

### ORNAMENTAL FLOWERS

Ornamental flowers are plants that exist in the wild but are often grown for how they look. They are popular for their colorful and often fragrant flowers and because they may attract butterflies and birds. Lilies, azaleas, angel's trumpets, and oleander are also common ornamental flowers.

# CORAL BEAN *(ERYTHRINA HERBACEA)*

The coral bean is a low shrub or small tree with leaves that are triangular-shaped. Its branches and trunk are covered in small thorns. Coral bean flowers are tube-shaped and bright red. They bloom around tall stalks in a unique long, tube-like shape. The coral bean gets its name from the bright red, bean-like seeds that appear in pods after its flowers have faded. Although the coral bean plant attracts hummingbirds, it is toxic to humans and pets. It can cause paralysis if ingested.

**FUN FACT**
Many American Indian groups have traditionally used parts of the coral bean to make medicine for different ailments.

## HOW TO SPOT

**Size:** Up to 16 feet (4.9 m) tall
**Flower:** Red, up to 8 inches (20.3 cm) long
**Fruit:** Seed pods with bright red seeds, 0.1 inches (0.3 cm) long
**Habitat:** Open woods with sandy soils
**Range:** Southeastern and central southwestern United States and northeastern Mexico

# DAFFODIL *(NARCISSUS PSEUDONARCISSUS)*

Daffodils grow from bulbs and have tall, waxy, blade-like leaves emerging upright from the base of the plant. Daffodil flowers bloom on a long stalk and often droop. They are usually yellow or white with a tube called a corona in the center. The corona is often longer than the petals and looks like a trumpet. All parts of the daffodil plant are toxic to humans and animals. Eating it can cause severe mouth irritation and vomiting.

## HOW TO SPOT

**Size:** 1.5 feet (0.5 m) tall

**Flower:** Yellow or white, very long corona, 4 inches (10.2 cm) in diameter

**Habitat:** Woodlands, grasslands, riverbanks, and rocky terrain

**Range:** Southern Canada and east and west coasts of United States, stretching west to Missouri

# FOXGLOVE *(DIGITALIS PURPUREA)*

The foxglove plant has hairy leaves that grow mid-way up its stem in a spiral shape. Its hanging flowers are usually purple, with a distinctive long bell shape and many spots on the inside of the petals. This flower shape attracts hummingbirds and especially bees. Bees can rest on the lip of the petals or climb inside the flower. All parts of the plant are toxic and even potentially fatal to humans and animals if ingested because they affect the heart.

## HOW TO SPOT

**Size:** 3 to 5 feet (0.9 to 1.5 m) tall
**Habitat:** Temperate woodlands, dry pastures, and rocky terrain
**Flower:** Purple, 2 to 3 inches (5.1 to 7.6 cm) long
**Range:** Northeastern and western North America

**FUN FACT**
One foxglove plant can produce one to two million tiny seeds.

# HYACINTH *(HYACINTHUS ORIENTALIS)*

The hyacinth plant grows from bulbs. It has sword-shaped leaves and small, star-shaped flowers surrounding a central stem. These flowers have an intense fragrance and are usually blue or violet. Hyacinth plants contain a substance called oxalic acid, which causes severe burns. All parts of the plant are toxic to humans and animals. It can cause skin burns if handled and severe internal burns if ingested. Ingestion can be fatal.

## HOW TO SPOT

**Size:** 0.7 to 1 foot (0.2 to 0.3 m) tall

**Flower:** Various colors, clusters are 4 to 6 inches (10.2 to 15.2 cm) long

**Habitat:** Woodlands, meadows, and rocky terrain

**Range:** Southern Canada, across the United States and central Mexico

# HYDRANGEA *(HYDRANGEA MACROPHYLLA)*

The hydrangea shrub produces abundant leaves and large clusters of flowers on upright stems. Its leaves are dark green and wedge-shaped, with teeth and very pointy ends. Individual flowers are small, but a cluster can contain more than 100 flowers. Hydrangea flowers come in many colors. All parts of the plant are poisonous to humans and animals. They can cause vomiting, diarrhea, and respiratory failure. Ingestion can be fatal in severe cases.

**FUN FACT**

A more acidic soil will produce blue hydrangea flowers, while soils with less acid produce pink ones.

## HOW TO SPOT

**Size:** 3 to 6 feet (0.9 to 1.8 m) tall

**Flower:** Various colors, clusters 2 to 4.75 inches (5.1 to 12.1 cm) long

**Habitat:** Woodlands, meadows, stream banks, and rocky terrain

**Range:** Across North America

# IRIS *(IRIS GERMANICA)*

The iris is a flowering plant that comes in many colors. It has tall, stiff, upright leaves shaped like swords or fans. Iris flowers have two types of petals. Upright petals are called standards, and drooping petals are called falls. The falls have fuzzy sections called beards. Iris flowers are fragrant and are often used in perfumes. The entire plant is poisonous to humans and animals. It most often causes skin irritation, mouth ulcers, diarrhea, and vomiting.

## FUN FACT

Irises can be almost any color. Their beards are sometimes a different color from the rest of the plant to help attract bees and other pollinators.

## HOW TO SPOT

**Size:** 2 to 4 feet (0.6 to 1.2 m) tall

**Flower:** Many colors, three standards and three falls with beards, 2 to 2.8 inches (5.1 to 7.1 cm) long

**Habitat:** Woodlands, meadows, and wetlands

**Range:** Across Canada and the United States

# TULIP *(TULIPA)*

Tulips grow from bulbs. They produce large, often bright flowers in every color except blue. Tulips bloom as a single flower at the top of a long stem. Their flowers are upright with a distinctive bell or cup shape, and they are not scented. Tulips have long, pointed, waxy leaves that grow from the base of the stem. The stems, leaves, roots and especially the bulbs of tulips are toxic to humans and animals. They can cause vomiting, diarrhea, and seizures.

## HOW TO SPOT

**Size:** 1.5 to 2 feet (0.5 to 0.6 m) tall

**Flower:** Many possible colors, six petals usually present, 3 to 6 inches (7.6 to 15.2 cm) tall

**Habitat:** Grasslands and rocky terrain

**Range:** Ontario, parts of the northeastern United States, Washington State, and California

# AMERICAN HOLLY *(ILEX OPACA)*

American holly is a tall, woody evergreen tree. It keeps its leaves all year round. Its limbs form a pyramid shape to the top of the tree. Its leaves are spiny but fragrant, with sharp points on the edges and well-defined central veins. American holly trees produce small, greenish-white flowers. However, American holly is better known for its clusters of small, red, round berries. These holly berries are poisonous to humans, cats, and dogs, causing digestive problems if ingested.

## HOW TO SPOT

**Size:** 60 feet (18.3 m) tall
**Fruit:** Red berries, 0.25 to 0.5 inches (0.6 to 1.3 cm) in diameter
**Habitat:** Mountainous areas, flood plains, coastlines, and river valleys
**Range:** Eastern and central United States

# AMERICAN MISTLETOE

## *(PHORADENDRON LEUCARPUM)*

American mistletoe grows on a host tree that provides it with nutrients, so it is a parasitic plant. It often forms a ball shape and tends to grow high in its hosts' branches. Its leaves are leathery and thick, growing in opposite pairs along their stems. American mistletoe has clusters of small, round, white berries. These berries are covered in a sticky, sap-like substance that is toxic to humans. It causes skin irritation and digestive upset.

### HOW TO SPOT

**Size:** Balls of stems and leaves up to 5 feet (1.5 m) wide

**Fruit:** White berries, 0.1 to 0.2 inches (0.3 to 0.5 cm) in diameter

**Habitat:** Tall deciduous trees, as a parasite

**Range:** Central and southern United States and Northern Mexico

# CASTOR BEAN *(RICINUS COMMUNIS)*

The castor bean plant has very wide, palm-shaped, abundant leaves with deep lobes and coarse teeth. Its leaves sometimes have a reddish tinge. It produces small flowers without petals, only many tiny stamens. Its seeds are shaped like shiny, brown beans. The seeds grow inside green or red pods covered in spikes. Castor bean seeds contain ricin, one of the deadliest toxins on Earth. Ingesting only a few seeds could kill an adult, causing fatal symptoms including vomiting, diarrhea, and seizures.

## HOW TO SPOT

**Size:** 6 to 10 feet (1.8 to 3 m) tall
**Fruit:** Seed pods with shiny, brown seeds, 0.5 inches (1.3 cm) long
**Habitat:** Riverbeds, fields, and disturbed areas
**Range:** Central and southwestern United States

## ORNAMENTAL SHRUBS AND PLANTS

Ornamental plants are often grown deliberately for decoration, but they exist in the wild too. They can provide structure and cover to landscape design. They are sometimes chosen for their size or their leaves. Some species of ornamental shrubs are poisonous.

# ELEPHANT EAR *(COLOCASIA ESCULENTA)*

The elephant ear plant is a shrub with huge, abundant leaves shaped like large arrows. Their tips point down, and their edges are often wavy. The leaves resemble the ears of elephants. Elephant ears are also commonly called taro plants for their corm, a large, bulb-like underground stem that is edible when cooked. But all parts of the plant are toxic to humans and animals when eaten raw. Ingestion can cause burning pain in the mouth and severe digestive upset.

**FUN FACT**

The taro plant's corm is an important food source in some parts of the world, but only when cooked and never raw. It is starchy, like a potato.

## HOW TO SPOT

**Size:** 3 to 6 feet (0.9 to 1.8 m) tall

**Leaves:** Up to 3 feet (0.9 m) long and 2 feet (0.6 m) wide

**Habitat:** Wetlands, coastal areas, and along rivers and streams

**Range:** Southeastern United States and the Gulf coast of Mexico

# RHUBARB *(RHEUM RHABARBARUM)*

Rhubarb is a colorful plant with bright green leaves and bright red stalks. Its leaves grow in clumps and are heart- or palm-shaped. The leaves have deep veins and curling edges. Rhubarb stems are thick and fleshy like celery. They are edible when cooked and popular in jams and pies. However, the stalk is the only edible part of the plant, and rhubarb leaves are poisonous to humans and animals. If ingested, they can affect the kidneys and cause nausea and difficulty breathing.

## HOW TO SPOT

**Size:** Up to 5 feet (1.5 m) tall
**Leaves:** Up to 2 feet (0.6 m) wide
**Habitat:** Fields, roadsides, and disturbed land
**Range:** Across Canada and the northern and central United States

# SAGO PALM *(CYCAS REVOLUTA)*

The sago palm is a short tree with a thick, rough, shaggy trunk. Sago palm leaves arch upward, growing in a circle around the top of the trunk, like a crown. Each leaf is made up of many thin blades that curve backward at the ends. The flowers do not have petals and look like large, golden pinecones. All parts of the plant are poisonous to humans and animals, especially the seeds. Sago palms contain toxins that can cause paralysis and damage the liver.

## HOW TO SPOT

**Size:** 3 to 10 feet (0.9 to 3 m) tall and wide

**Leaves:** 3 to 7 feet (0.9 to 2.1 m) long

**Habitat:** Tropical and subtropical areas with sandy soils

**Range:** California and the southeastern United States, especially Florida

### FUN FACT

Sago palms are a prehistoric plant that predate even the dinosaurs. A sago palm plant can live for more than 200 years.

# AMERICAN POKEWEED

## *(PHYTOLACCA AMERICANA)*

American pokeweed is tall with bright green, wavy-edged leaves. The leaves have an unpleasant odor when crushed. This plant has small, white flowers that are replaced by round berries that ripen from green to shiny black. They grow on drooping, bright red or purple stems. The entire plant is poisonous to humans, pets, and livestock. Toxins can be absorbed through the skin or through eating. They cause diarrhea and vomiting.

### HOW TO SPOT

**Size:** 4 to 10 feet (1.2 to 3 m) tall
**Fruit:** Purple-black berries, 0.3 to 0.4 inches (0.8 to 1 cm) in diameter
**Habitat:** Pastures, woodlands, cleared land, and wastelands
**Range:** Southeastern Canada and the midwestern, eastern, and southern United States

### WHAT ARE POKEWEEDS?

Pokeweeds are flowering plants that produce distinctive black berries on bright red or purplish-red stems. All parts of pokeweed plants are poisonous when handled or ingested.

# INDIAN POKEWEED

## *(PHYTOLACCA ACINOSA)*

Indian pokeweed is a flowering plant with large, spear-shaped, bright green leaves with smooth edges. Its flowers are small and green or white. In late summer, its black berries appear on bright red or purple stems. These berries are not round like those of the American pokeweed. They have many chambers that looked like curved bumps. Indian pokeweeds attract birds, but they are poisonous to humans and other mammals. They can cause vomiting and diarrhea.

### HOW TO SPOT

**Size:** 3 to 4 feet (0.9 to 1.2 m) tall

**Fruit:** Dark purple or black berries with many chambers, 0.3 inches (0.8 cm) in diameter

**Habitat:** Pastures, woodlands, cleared land, and wastelands

**Range:** Southeastern Canada through the midwestern and southern United States

# CALIFORNIA POPPY

## *(ESCHSCHOLZIA CALIFORNICA)*

Native to California and northeastern Mexico, the California poppy is also called the golden poppy. It has blue-green, fern-like leaves with a feathery look. Its single cup-shaped flowers bloom on top of the stem and have four silky petals. They are usually bright orange but can also be yellow or red. The California poppy is poisonous because it contains toxins that affect the nervous system and causes dizziness, drowsiness, and vomiting, especially in children and pets.

### HOW TO SPOT

**Size:** 0.4 to 1 foot (0.1 to 0.3 m) tall

**Flower:** Orange, 2 to 4 inches (5.1 to 10.2 cm) in diameter

**Habitat:** Hillsides, plains, and mountainous regions

**Range:** Across the United States and northwestern Mexico

### WHAT ARE POPPIES?

Poppies include over 120 species of plants that come in many different sizes and a wide range of bright colors. A single flower usually blooms on each stem in a cup shape, with four to six petals. They close at night and open again in the sunlight. Poppies can be poisonous when eaten.

# CELANDINE POPPY

## *(STYLOPHORUM DIPHYLLUM)*

The celandine poppy has abundant light green leaves that grow in clumps around its base and in pairs near the top of the stem. Small, single, cup-shaped flowers appear on each stem. They are brilliant yellow, with four petals and many yellow or orange stamens. After flowering, the plants develop small seed pods with long white hairs. Ingesting the celandine poppy can irritate the digestive system in humans and animals. The thick sap can burn the skin and eyes.

### HOW TO SPOT

**Size:** 1 to 1.5 feet (0.3 to 0.5 m) tall

**Flower:** Bright yellow, 1 to 2 inches (2.5 to 5.1 cm) in diameter

**Habitat:** Moist forests and woodlands

**Range:** Southeastern Canada and the eastern United States

# ICELAND POPPY *(PAPAVER NUDICAULE)*

The Iceland poppy has bright green, feathery leaves. The leaves have deep lobes that grow in clumps at the base of the plant. Its stems are curved at the top and hairy, with a single wide, cup-shaped flower. The flowers are large and saucer-shaped. They are a variety of colors, with crinkled, papery petals and a light fragrance. Iceland poppies are attractive to honeybees and bumblebees but poisonous to mammals. Ingesting them can cause digestive irritation. Handling them can irritate the skin and eyes.

**FUN FACT**

**Despite their name, Iceland poppies do not grow in Iceland.**

## HOW TO SPOT

**Size:** 1 to 2 feet (0.3 to 0.6 m) tall

**Flower:** Various colors, 2 to 3 inches (5.1 to 7.6 cm) in diameter

**Habitat:** Rocky areas with colder climates

**Range:** Southern Canada and the northern United States

# MEXICAN TULIP POPPY

## *(HUNNEMANNIA FUMARIIFOLIA)*

The Mexican tulip poppy has small, single yellow flowers with many short stamens. These stamens have orange antlers. The flowers have four petals that overlap into a cup shape and resemble open tulips. Their leaves are gray-green and abundant, with deep lobes that give them a feathery appearance. Their stems are woody at the base. Mexican tulip poppies can cause digestive upset if ingested.

### HOW TO SPOT

**Size:** Up to 2 feet (0.6 m) tall

**Flower:** Bright yellow, 2 to 3 inches (5.1 to 7.6 cm) in diameter.

**Habitat:** Desert regions, rocky areas, high elevations, and disturbed lands

**Range:** Southwestern United States and northern and central Mexico

# CREEPING SPURGE

## *(EUPHORBIA MYRSINITES)*

Creeping spurge is a spreading plant that grows low to the ground. It is often considered a harmful invasive weed. Its leaves are fleshy, waxy, and blue-green, growing in tight spirals around sprawling stems. Creeping spurge produces bright yellow bracts that look like small flowers. It causes vomiting and diarrhea if ingested. Its sap can burn the skin and cause blindness if it gets in the eyes.

### HOW TO SPOT

**Size:** 4 to 12 inches (10.2 to 30.5 cm) tall

**Leaves:** 0.1 to 0.4 inches (0.3 to 1 cm) long; 0.1 to 0.2 inches (0.3 to 0.5 cm) wide

**Habitat:** Rocky terrain, grasslands, and disturbed areas

**Range:** Widespread in southwestern Canada, the United States, and Mexico

### WHAT ARE SPURGES?

Spurges have specialized leaves called bracts. They participate in reproduction as well as photosynthesis. These bracts often come in interesting colors and shapes. Many species of spurge are considered fast-growing weeds.

# CROWN OF THORNS *(EUPHORBIA MILII)*

The crown of thorns is a tall, sprawling spurge whose branches and stems hold water. They are covered in sharp black thorns, giving the plant its common name. The plant's leaves are oval and fleshy, and its stems are woody at the base. Crown of thorn plants have bright red or pink bracts that look like flowers. They produce sap that can burn the skin and eyes. Ingesting the plant can cause digestive upset in humans and serious illness in pets and livestock.

## HOW TO SPOT

**Size:** Up to 6 feet (1.8 m) tall

**Bracts:** Bright red bracts in opposite pairs, 0.5 inches (1.3 cm) in diameter

**Habitat:** Rocky areas, coastal areas, forests, and disturbed areas

**Range:** Southern United States and Mexico

# LEAFY SPURGE *(EUPHORBIA ESULA)*

The leafy spurge is a succulent shrub. It has tall, branched stems and thin, narrow, blade-like leaves. When broken, its leaves and stems are filled with a milky sap that is toxic to humans and animals. This sap can cause skin burns and irritate the eyes. The plant's green or yellowish heart-shaped bracts look like petals. Leafy spurge is an aggressive and invasive plant. If ingested, it can cause vomiting.

**FUN FACT**

**Goats are able to eat leafy spurge safely and may be able to help remove it.**

## HOW TO SPOT

**Size:** 1 to 2.5 feet (0.3 to 0.8 m) tall

**Leaves:** 1 to 4 inches (2.5 to 10.2 cm) long; 0.3 to 0.5 inches (0.8 to 1.3 cm) wide

**Habitat:** Prairies, fields, and disturbed areas

**Range:** Widespread across Canada and the United States

# SPOTTED SPURGE

## *(EUPHORBIA MACULATA)*

The spotted spurge is a small weed that grows along the ground and produces small, greenish-white flowers. Spotted spurge gets its name from the reddish or purplish splotches in the middle of its leaves. These leaves grow in opposite pairs and are shaped like long ovals. When torn, they produce a milky sap that causes skin rashes. Ingesting the plant is also toxic to humans, pets, and livestock and can cause stomach upset.

### HOW TO SPOT

**Size:** 3 to 12 inches (7.6 to 30.5 cm) tall
**Leaves:** 0.2 to 0.7 inches (0.5 to 1.8 cm) long
**Habitat:** Wetlands and woodlands; grows well anywhere with disturbed areas with compacted soil
**Range:** Widespread across North America

# ATLANTIC POISON OAK

## *(TOXICODENDRON PUBESCENS)*

The Atlantic poison oak shrub has long, prominent leaves that are veined. These leaves are usually hairy, with broad, jagged teeth. The leaves appear in distinctive groups of three. They are glossy and usually green but can turn orange or yellow in the fall. All parts of the Atlantic poison oak plant are poisonous and cause severe skin irritation. Handling the plant or even contaminated clothing can result in a severe, itchy, burning rash with blisters.

### HOW TO SPOT

**Size:** Up to 3 feet (0.9 m) tall
**Leaves:** 2 to 8 inches (5.1 to 20.3 cm) long; 0.75 to 5 inches (1.9 to 12.7 cm) wide
**Habitat:** Forests, woodlands, fields, and sandy areas
**Range:** Central and southern United States

### WHAT ARE SUMACS?

The sumac family is also called the cashew family. It includes plants that produce edible fruits and nuts, such as cashew and mango trees. However, sumacs such as poison oak and poison ivy plants can be harmful and cause severe skin irritation.

# POISON IVY *(TOXICODENDRON RADICANS)*

As a vine, poison ivy can trail along the ground or climb around trees. Its leaves are often broad and tear-shaped. They are usually smooth and glossy, but some plants have leaves with jagged teeth at the edges. The green leaves become red in the fall. Poison ivy leaves appear in groups of three. The middle leaf in each group is the longest because it has a longer stem. Poison ivy causes painful, itching, burning rashes that may blister the skin.

## HOW TO SPOT

**Size:** Up to 5 feet (1.5 m) tall as a shrub, longer than 150 feet (45.7 m) as a vine

**Leaves:** Groups of three, 2 to 8 inches (5.1 to 20.3 cm) long; 0.8 to 5 inches (2 to 12.7 cm) wide

**Habitat:** Woodlands, clearings, and disturbed areas

**Range:** Southern Canada and throughout the United States

## FUN FACT

**Because their leaves appear in groups of three, a popular saying about avoiding poison ivy and poison oak is, "Leaves of three, let it be."**

# POISON SUMAC *(TOXICODENDRON VERNIX)*

Poison sumac is a sumac shrub whose leaves do not appear in groups of three. Instead, it has groups of seven to thirteen oval-shaped leaves that grow on distinctive reddish stems. These leaves can also be reddish. They are shaped like long ovals with pointed tips and wavy edges. Poison sumac also produces clusters of creamy white berries that are poisonous if eaten. Handling poison sumac can also cause severe, painful skin rashes.

## HOW TO SPOT

**Size:** Up to 30 feet (9.1 m) tall

**Leaves:** 2 to 4 inches (5.1 to 10.2 cm) long; 0.75 to 2 inches (1.9 to 5.1 cm) wide

**Habitat:** Wetlands, marshlands and coastal plains

**Range:** Southeastern Canada and the eastern United States

# WESTERN POISON OAK

## *(TOXICODENDRON DIVERSILOBUM)*

The western poison oak plant can be a shrub or a woody vine and has a widely varying length and height. Its leaves usually appear in groups of three. The leaves have prominent veins and deep lobes or teeth. These leaves are glossy and change color from bronze, to green, and finally bright red or pink in the fall. The leaves fall off in winter. Western poison oak has a milky sap that can cause severe skin rashes.

### HOW TO SPOT

**Size:** 1.5 to 13 feet (0.5 to 4 m) tall or 10 to 30 feet (3 to 9.1 m) long as a vine

**Leaves:** 2 to 8 inches (5.1 to 20.3 cm) long; 0.75 to 5 inches (1.9 to 12.7 cm) wide

**Habitat:** Forests, woodlands, and grasslands

**Range:** Western North America

# MILK THISTLE *(SILYBUM MARIANUM)*

The milk thistle is an upright, flowering plant. It is considered an invasive weed in some areas. It has the purple, downy flowers characteristic of many thistle plants. Its leaves surround the flower and are shaped like spiky blades with white marbling. Milk thistle is used in some medicines, but its thorns and leaves have a toxin that can cause stomach upset and allergic reactions when eaten. It is also toxic to sheep and cattle.

## HOW TO SPOT

**Size:** 1 to 6.5 feet (0.3 to 2 m) tall

**Flower:** Purple and spiny, 2 inches (5.1 cm) in diameter

**Habitat:** Meadows, pastures, disturbed land, and urban land

**Range:** Southern and eastern Canada and the northern United States

## WHAT ARE THISTLES?

Thistles are small, flowering plants often considered weeds. They are characterized by fuzzy flowers and spiky, thorny leaves and stems. Different species of thistle can be toxic.

# YELLOW STAR THISTLE

## *(CENTAUREA SOLSTITIALIS)*

The yellow star thistle gets its common name from the circle of long, pointy spines that are shaped like a star around its flowers. It is an upright plant with flowers made up of downy, yellow spikes. Its branching stems and toothless leaves are both hairy, with a gray-green color. Yellow star thistle is especially toxic to horses, who can develop a serious neurological disorder after eating it.

**FUN FACT**

Yellow star thistle is an invasive weed that is estimated to have infested over 15 million acres in the American West.

## HOW TO SPOT

**Size:** 2 to 5 feet (0.6 to 1.5 m) tall

**Flower:** Yellow, 0.6 inches (1.5 cm) in diameter; spines 1 to 2 inches (2.5 to 5.1 cm) long

**Habitat:** Pastures, open fields, grasslands, and disturbed lands

**Range:** Widespread across North America

# ENGLISH IVY *(HEDERA HELIX)*

The English ivy plant is a woody vine that can climb very high or spread along the ground. It spreads aggressively and can easily become invasive and prevent other plants from growing. English ivy has heart-shaped, dark green, wavy leaves with white veins. Mature plants produce dark purple berries that look like grapes. The leaves and berries are poisonous. They can cause digestive and respiratory problems and even coma in large enough doses.

## HOW TO SPOT

**Size:** 66 to 98 feet (20.1 to 29.9 m) when climbing

**Leaves:** 4 inches (10.2 cm) long and 2.5 to 5 inches (6.4 to 12.7 cm) wide

**Habitat:** Woodlands and disturbed areas

**Range:** Widespread across North America

## WHAT ARE VINES?

A vine is a type of plant that either trails along the ground or climbs up a sturdy structure such as a tree, wall, or fence for support. Many species of vines can be invasive.

# PURPLE LANTANA

## *(LANTANA MONTEVIDENSIS)*

The purple lantana plant is a vine that trails along the ground or climbs trees or other structures. The dark green leaves are arrow-shaped. These leaves have pointed tips, and many teeth. They produce a strong odor when crushed, and they can irritate the skin when touched. The fragrant flowers are usually lavender with yellow centers. Its clusters of berries can be reddish or purple. Lantana leaves and berries cause vomiting, diarrhea, and liver failure, especially in livestock.

**FUN FACT**

***Lantana montevidensis* attracts bees, butterflies, and hummingbirds.**

### HOW TO SPOT

**Size:** 1 to 2 feet (0.3 to 0.6 m) tall and up to 10 feet (3 m) wide

**Flower:** Lavender or pink, in clusters up to 1.5 inches ( 3.8 cm) across

**Habitat:** Dry, sandy soils and hot regions

**Range:** Southern United States and Mexico

# ROSARY PEA *(ABRUS PRECATORIUS)*

The rosary pea is an invasive, flowering vine from the bean family. It can sprawl along the ground or climb high around trees or other structures. It has smooth, oval-shaped leaves in pairs along each side of the stem. Its flowers are small, white to pinkish-purple, and they grow in clusters. The rosary pea's long, oval seed pods hold many seeds that are usually glossy red with black tips, like ladybugs. They are extremely poisonous, and eating even one can kill an adult person.

**FUN FACT**

The glossy, bean-like seeds of the rosary pea are used to make bracelets, necklaces, and rosaries.

## HOW TO SPOT

**Size:** 10 to 20 feet (3 to 6.1 m) when climbing
**Seeds:** Red with a black spot, 0.3 inches (0.8 cm) long
**Habitat:** Woodlands, coastal areas, disturbed areas
**Range:** Florida and parts of Alabama and Georgia

# YELLOW JESSAMINE

## *(GELSEMIUM SEMPERVIRENS)*

This flowering vine has dark green, arrow-shaped leaves that have sharply pointed tips. Its flowers are bright yellow and grow in clusters. They are trumpet-shaped and very fragrant. The flowers produce nectar that is toxic to honeybees but beneficial to bumblebees. All parts of the yellow jessamine plant are poisonous and can kill livestock. Humans have also been poisoned by mistaking the plant for honeysuckle. Symptoms include vomiting, blurry vision, difficulty breathing, heart problems, seizures, and coma.

### HOW TO SPOT

**Size:** 10 to 20 feet (3 to 6.1 m) when climbing
**Flower:** Bright yellow, 1 to 1.5 inches (2.5 to 3.8 cm) long
**Habitat:** Woodlands and meadows
**Range:** Southern United States and Mexico

# COMMON BUTTONBUSH

## *(CEPHALANTHUS OCCIDENTALIS)*

This small shrub has long, broad, oval leaves with pointed tips. They are glossy with smooth edges and appear in pairs or groups of three. Common buttonbush flower clusters look like round, white pincushions because they are covered in pointy styles. All parts of the common buttonbush plant can cause vomiting, muscle spasms, and paralysis.

### HOW TO SPOT

**Size:** 5 to 8 feet (1.5 to 2.4 m) tall
**Flower:** 1 to 1.5 inches (2.5 to 3.8 cm) in diameter
**Habitat:** Wetlands and moist woods
**Range:** Eastern Canada and widespread in the United States

### WHAT ARE WETLAND PLANTS?

Wetland plants thrive in wetland habitats. Wetlands are areas like marshes or swamps that are covered in shallow water or have very wet soil that does not drain water well.

# NORTH AMERICAN WATER LILY

## *(NYMPHAEA ODORATA)*

This floating plant has round leaves called lily pads. Lily pads are wide and circular with a V-shaped notch. North American water lilies have very fragrant flowers that open during the daytime but close at night. They have many white, pointed petals that curve up. The flowers have up to 40 yellow stamens. The flowers and leaves have separate stems underwater. Although the flowers are edible, they can have sedative effects and cause digestive issues if ingested in large doses.

### HOW TO SPOT

**Size:** 16 inches (40.6 cm) tall

**Flower:** White or pink, with 20 to 30 pointed petals, 3 to 6 inches (7.6 to 15.2 cm) in diameter

**Habitat:** Lakes, ponds, swamps, and slow streams

**Range:** Across southern Canada and the United States

# PENNYROYAL *(MENTHA PULEGIUM)*

The pennyroyal plant's stem can be upright or low to the ground. It has many narrow oval leaves with small, widely spaced teeth. Its stems can be green or reddish-purple and are sometimes hairy. Pennyroyal flowers grow in clusters. They are purple and very small. They grow in dense whorls and have very long stamens that give them a hairy look. Pennyroyal produces an oil that is poisonous even in small doses and fatal in large doses. It can cause vomiting, dizziness, and organ failure.

## HOW TO SPOT

**Size:** 16 inches (40.6 cm) tall

**Flower:** Purple, with long stamens, 0.3 inches (0.8 cm) long and wide

**Habitat:** Damp meadows, ponds, and streams

**Range:** Eastern and central Canada and the United States

# SOUTHERN SWAMP LILY

## *(CRINUM AMERICANUM)*

The southern swamp lily grows in small groups and thrives in still water. It has long, glossy, upright green leaves shaped like blades. Its flowers have a spider-like appearance. They are bright white or pinkish with pink or red stalks. Their six long, narrow petals curve downward, but their long, purple stamens curve upward. Southern swamp lily flowers are very fragrant and attract moths at night. Ingesting any part of the plant can cause stomach pain, vomiting, and diarrhea.

### HOW TO SPOT

**Size:** 2 to 4 feet (0.6 to 1.2 m) tall; 1 to 2 feet (0.3 to 0.6 m) wide

**Flower:** White or pink, 4 to 6 inches (10.2 to 15.2 cm) long and 0.5 inches (1.3 cm) wide

**Habitat:** Swamps, marshes, and stream banks

**Range:** Southeastern United States and Mexico

# WATER HEMLOCK *(CICUTA MACULATA)*

The water hemlock plant is one of the deadliest in North America. It has upright, hollow, branching stems with many long, arrow-shaped leaflets. Its leaves are pointed with many teeth and prominent veins. Water hemlock produces many tiny white flowers in umbrella-shaped clusters. It can cause serious and life-threatening symptoms in humans within 30 to 60 minutes of being ingested. Water hemlock poisoning causes abdominal pain, vomiting, convulsions, seizures, brain damage, and often death.

## HOW TO SPOT

**Size:** Up to 8 feet (2.4 m) tall
**Flower:** White, 2 to 5 inches (5.1 to 12.7 cm) in diameter
**Habitat:** Swamps, marshes, stream banks, and wet meadows
**Range:** Throughout North America

## FUN FACT

The black swallowtail butterfly lays its eggs on water hemlock plants. The larvae eat the leaves.

# WATER LETTUCE *(PISTIA STRATIOTES)*

Water lettuce is an invasive floating plant that looks very similar to a head of lettuce. It has thick gray-green leaves with white veins. The hairy leaves grow in a circular pattern like a rose, called a rosette. Water lettuce also has long underwater roots that are white or tan and look feathery. It produces tiny flowers with a spathe and spadix in the center of the rosette, but they can be difficult to see. Water lettuce is poisonous if ingested. It causes vomiting, diarrhea, and swelling of the lips, tongue, and throat.

**FUN FACT**

**Large clumps of water lettuce plants can block waterways and lower water quality, killing fish.**

## HOW TO SPOT

**Size:** 3 to 6 inches (7.6 to 15.2 cm) tall
**Leaves:** 6 inches (15.2 cm) long
**Habitat:** Ponds, ditches, and swamps
**Range:** Widespread in the United States

# CANADIAN YEW *(TAXUS CANADENSIS)*

The Canadian yew is a woody, sprawling shrub with spreading branches. Its needles are flat and dark green on top but pale green underneath. They turn reddish-brown in winter. The Canadian yew produces cones that look like bright red berries. They have an open circle at the end, where a single seed is visible. Canadian yews are not toxic to birds, but all parts are poisonous to humans and other animals if ingested. They can cause severe vomiting and affect the heart rate.

## HOW TO SPOT

**Size:** 3 to 5 feet (0.9 to 1.5 m) tall; 8 feet (2.4 m) wide
**Fruit:** Red, berry-like cone with a brown seed, 0.25 to 0.5 inches (0.6 to 1.3 cm) long
**Habitat:** Wetland areas and moist forests
**Range:** Eastern Canada and the northeastern and central United States

## WHAT ARE YEWS?

Yews are shrubs and small trees with short, straight green leaves called needles. Female yew trees produce red, fleshy cones that look like berries. All parts of the yew are poisonous if ingested.

# PACIFIC YEW OR WESTERN YEW

## *(TAXUS BREVIFOLIA)*

The Pacific yew usually appears as woody shrubs in drier areas and small trees in areas with more moisture. It has scaly red or purplish-brown bark and flat, dark green needles densely spiraled around the stem. Its single seeds are covered in cones that look like bright red, fleshy berries with open ends. Pacific yews are very poisonous if ingested, especially the seeds. Many parts of the plant can cause vomiting, seizures, confusion, and even death.

**FUN FACT**

**Pacific yew trees produce a very strong wood that is used to make furniture, cabinetry, and canoe paddles.**

**HOW TO SPOT**

**Size:** 6 to 12 feet (1.8 to 3.7 m) tall

**Fruit:** Red, berry-like cone with one seed, 0.5 inches (1.3 cm) long

**Habitat:** Forests, stream banks, and shady flatlands

**Range:** Western Canada and the western United States

# FALSE HELLEBORE *(VERATRUM VIRIDE)*

Also called Indian poke or corn lily, the false hellebore is a small, upright plant. It has broad, bright green leaves growing in a spiral shape. These leaves have noticeably heavy ribbing, with rounded sides and pointed tips. False hellebores produce long branches of many tiny, yellow-green flowers. All parts of the plant are poisonous, especially the leaves and roots. Ingesting them can cause vomiting, abdominal pain, and heart problems that can be fatal in some cases.

## HOW TO SPOT

**Size:** 2 to 6 feet (0.6 to 1.8 m) tall

**Leaves:** 1 foot (0.3 m) long; 6 inches (15.2 cm) wide

**Habitat:** Wetlands, moist meadows, and open forests at high elevation

**Range:** Southwestern and southeastern Canada and the northern United States

# GIANT HOGWEED

## *(HERACLEUM MANTEGAZZIANUM)*

Giant hogweed is a flowering plant that grows very tall with huge leaves. These leaves are palm-shaped with teeth and deep lobes. They are abundant at the base of the plant. Giant hogweeds have thick stems with distinctive purple spots and white hairs. They produce very large, umbrella-shaped clusters of small white flowers. The sap of giant hogweed causes extreme sun sensitivity in humans. It can harm the eyes and cause painful blisters and scarring of the skin.

### HOW TO SPOT

**Size:** Up to 20 feet (6.1 m) tall

**Flower:** White or greenish-white clusters up to 2.5 feet (0.8 m) in diameter

**Habitat:** Wetlands, woodlands, and fields

**Range:** Western and eastern Canada, northwestern and northeastern United States

# MAYAPPLE *(PODOPHYLLUM PELTATUM)*

Mayapples grow in clusters and have round leaves with deep lobes that look like umbrellas above the plant's single white flower. The flowers nod downward and have many stamens with yellow antlers. Their fruit matures from green to yellow and looks like small lemons. All parts of the mayapple plant are extremely poisonous and can cause serious symptoms such as skin rashes when handled and vomiting, diarrhea, confusion, paralysis, and even death when ingested.

## HOW TO SPOT

**Size:** 1 to 1.5 feet (0.3 to 0.5 m) tall
**Flower:** White, 2 to 3 inches (5.1 to 7.6 cm) in diameter
**Habitat:** Woodlands, fields, and riverbanks
**Range:** Eastern and central North America

# MOUNTAIN LAUREL *(KALMIA LATIFOLIA)*

Mountain laurel can grow especially tall on mountain slopes. This shrub's dark green leaves are broad and glossy, with smooth edges and prominent center veins. The flowers grow in clusters, with pointy-tipped petals forming hexagon shapes. The flowers are white or light pink with a pattern of darker pink spots. All parts of the mountain laurel, including its pollen and honey made by bees using this nectar, are poisonous to humans and animals. When ingested, they can cause vomiting, breathing and heart problems, paralysis, and even death.

**FUN FACT**
Mountain laurel is the state flower of Connecticut.

## HOW TO SPOT

**Size:** 10 to 30 feet (3 to 9.1 m) tall

**Flower:** White or pink and spotted, clusters 4 to 6 inches (10.2 to 15.2 cm) in diameter

**Habitat:** Rocky areas, mountain slopes, and woodlands

**Range:** Eastern and central United States

# SHOWY RATTLEBOX

## *(CROTALARIA SPECTABILIS)*

The showy rattlebox is an invasive flowering plant. It has long, oblong leaves with rounded tips, smooth edges, and center veins. They grow in opposite pairs along the stem. Showy rattlebox flowers grow in upright clusters. They are bright yellow, with round or oval petals and dark, reddish-purple lines at the base. All parts of the showy rattlebox plant are toxic to humans and animals, especially the seeds. Ingesting the plant can cause stomach problems and lower blood pressure and heart rate.

### HOW TO SPOT

**Size:** 2 to 5 feet (0.6 to 1.5 m) tall
**Flower:** Yellow, 1 inch (2.5 cm) in diameter
**Habitat:** Fields, pastures, and disturbed areas
**Range:** Southeastern United States

### FUN FACT

The name *rattlebox* comes from the rattling sound made by shaking the plant's dried seed pods.

# TANSY RAGWORT

## *(SENECIO JACOBAEA)*

Tansy ragwort has tall, straight, upright leaves with deep lobes and blunt ends. Its leaves have an unpleasant smell. The bright yellow flowers grow in large clusters. They have long, oval petals around a center of short, orange stamens. These flowers have a daisy-like shape. Tansy ragwort is poisonous when both fresh and dry. Ingesting tansy ragwort can cause swelling, inflammation, diarrhea, and liver damage.

**FUN FACT**

**One tansy ragwort plant can produce up to 2,500 flowers and 120,000 seeds.**

### HOW TO SPOT

**Size:** 0.7 to 4 feet (0.2 to 1.2 m) tall
**Flower:** Yellow, 1 inch (2.5 cm) in diameter
**Habitat:** Pastures, wetlands, and disturbed areas
**Range:** Southern Canada and the northern and central United States

# GLOSSARY

**abundant**
Existing in large quantities, plentiful.

**biodiversity**
The variety of animal and plant life in an environment.

**disturbed area**
Land with human-made changes to its surface.

**ecosystem**
A community of living organisms, including plants and animals.

**fatal**
Causing death.

**fragrant**
Having a pleasant smell.

**ingest**
To take in as food.

**invasive**
Plants that grow out of control and can damage the ecosystem.

**parasite**
An organism that lives on a host and takes its nutrients.

**pollinator**
An insect that carries pollen to allow fertilization.

**spadix**
A fleshy spike with many tiny flowers. Usually appears with a spathe.

**spathe**
A large bract or modified leaf that often looks like a petal surrounding the spadix.

**stamen**
The male fertilizing organ of a plant, usually with an antler.

**style**
A slender stalk that is part of the female reproductive system of a plant.

**succulent**
A plant with thick, fleshy leaves or stems adapted to storing water.

**teeth**
In plants, zigzags on the edges of leaves.

**toxic**
Able to cause harm.

**untoothed**
Describes plants without teeth on their edges.

**whorl**
A group of three or more leaves that encircle a plant's stem.

# TO LEARN MORE

## FURTHER READINGS

Carlson, Kit. *The Book of Killer Plants: A Field Guide to Nature's Deadliest Creations*. Cider Mill Press, 2022.

Meuninck, Jim. *Basic Illustrated Poisonous and Psychoactive Plants (Basic Illustrated Series)*. Falcon Guides, 2014.

Turner, Nancy J. and von Aderkas, Patrick. *The North American Guide to Poisonous Plants and Mushrooms*. Timber Press, 2009.

## ONLINE RESOURCES

To learn more about poisonous and deadly plants, please visit abdobooklinks.com or scan this QR code. These links are routinely monitored and updated to provide the most current information available.

# PHOTO CREDITS

Cover Photos: Chimperil59/iStock/Getty Images, front (American pokeweed); merlinpf/iStock/Getty Images, front (deadly nightshade); vencavolrab/iStock/Getty Images, front (milk thistle); leskas/iStock/Getty Images, front (white baneberry); Wildnerdpix/iStock/Getty Images, front (Big Bend bluebonnet); AlessandraRC/iStock/Getty Images, front (western poison oak); constantgardener/iStock/Getty Images, front (Iceland poppy); Chase D'animulls/Shutterstock, front (coral bean); Robert Winkler/iStock/Getty Images, front (Eastern skunk cabbage), back (North American water lily); Gordon Magee/iStock/Getty Images, front (Jack-in-the-pulpit); Saddako/iStock/Getty Images, front (Hydrangeas); Iva Vagnerova/Shutterstock, back (Indian pokeweed)
Interior Photos: Robert Winkler/iStock/Getty Images, 1 (top left), 95; LCBallard/iStock/Getty Images, 1 (top right), 5 (top left), 20, 51; Ed Reschke/Stone/Getty Images, 1 (middle), 76 (top), 85; KenWiedemann/iStock/Getty Images, 1 (bottom left), 14 (left); vencavolrab/iStock/Getty Images, 1 (bottom right), 88; sdominick/iStock/Getty Images, 4 (left), 38; PavloBaliukh/iStock/Getty Images, 4 (right), 62; Wirestock/iStock/Getty Images, 5 (top center), 102 (top); Iurii Garmash/iStock/Getty Images, 5 (top right), 9 (bottom); Chase D'animulls/iStock/Getty Images, 5 (bottom left), 34 (right), 61, 84; Sycikimagery/Moment/Getty Images, 5 (bottom right), 17 (top); Firdes Sayilan/Shutterstock, 8; Sunshower Shots/Shutterstock, 9 (top); Nowaczyk/Shutterstock, 10 (left); zhuclear/iStock/Getty Images, 10 (right), 19 (top); samuel howell/iStock/Getty Images, 11, 44, 46; carlofranco/iStock/Getty Images, 12; M Andy/Shutterstock, 13; Cynthia Shirk/iStock/Getty Images, 14 (right); Dewin ID/Shutterstock, 15; Brian Woolman/iStock/Getty Images, 16 (left), 27; W. de Vries/Shutterstock, 16 (right); Dee/iStock/Getty Images, 17 (bottom); wrangel/iStock/Getty Images, 18 (left); Design Pics/Robert Cable/Getty Images, 18 (right); S Marcum/Shutterstock, 19 (bottom); Edita Medeina/Shutterstock, 21; Sergey V Kalyakin/Shutterstock, 22; leskas/iStock/Getty Images, 23 (top); Richard Jackson/iStock/Getty Images, 23 (bottom); Wildnerdpix/iStock/Getty Images, 24 (left); David Jeffrey Ringer/Shutterstock, 24 (right); N8tureGrl/iStock/Getty Images, 25, 40 (left); Ronnie Wiggin/Moment/Getty Images, 26; ArgenLant/iStock/Getty Images, 28, 112 (top right); Al Bittler/Shutterstock, 29 (left); chapin31/iStock/Getty Images, 29 (right); Gleti/Shutterstock, 30; Oleg Kovtun Hydrobio/Shutterstock, 31; Piaffe Photography/Shutterstock, 32 (left); DE AGOSTINI PICTURE LIBRARY/Getty Images, 32 (right); mcajan/Shutterstock, 33 (top); Jeff Holcombe/Shutterstock, 33 (bottom); Sunshower Shots/iStock/Getty Images, 34 (left), 83; Anna Nelidova/iStock/Getty Images, 35 (top); Gerald Corsi/iStock/Getty Images, 35 (bottom), 47, 57 (top), 57 (bottom), 89; Tetra Images/Getty Images, 36; Tartezy/iStock/Getty Images, 37 (top); johnandersonphoto/iStock/Getty Images, 37 (bottom), 112 (bottom right); Shelly Bychowski Shots/Shutterstock, 39; Frank DeBonis/iStock/Getty Images, 40 (right); aimintang/iStock/Getty Images, 41, 78 (top); Antonel/iStock/Getty Images,

42 (left); Mihail2121/Shutterstock, 42 (right); APugach/Shutterstock, 43 (top); Sokor Space/Shutterstock, 43 (bottom); Anton Nikitinskiy/Shutterstock, 45; DavidPrahl/iStock/Getty Images, 48 (top); OGphoto/iStock/Getty Images, 48 (bottom); Karel Bock/iStock/Getty Images, 49; LucyF/iStock/Getty Images, 50; Sojib kh/Shutterstock, 52; David Graves/iStock/Getty Images, 53 (top); dadalia/iStock/Getty Images, 53 (bottom); Naturfoto Honal/ Corbis Documentary/Getty Images, 54 (top); arenysam/iStock/Getty Images, 54 (bottom); Pixiversal/Shutterstock, 55 (top); krolya25/Shutterstock, 55 (bottom); Mantonature/iStock/Getty Images, 56 (top); DeepDesertPhoto/RooM/Getty Images, 56 (bottom); Arkela/iStock/Getty Images, 58; Nick Pecker/Shutterstock, 59; nickkurzenko/iStock/Getty Images, 60; Melinda Podor/Moment/Getty Images, 63; sichkarenko.com/Shutterstock, 64 (top); Solidago/E+/Getty Images, 64 (bottom); azndc/iStock/Getty Images, 65 (top); Saddako/iStock/Getty Images, 65 (bottom); m-kojot/iStock/Getty Images, 66 (top); Stephen B. Goodwin/Shutterstock, 66 (bottom); kanonsky/iStock/Getty Images, 67; Molotok289/Shutterstock, 68 (top); huggy1/iStock/Getty Images, 68 (bottom); Christine_Kohler/iStock/Getty Images, 69; silkfactory/iStock/Getty Images, 70; komkrit Preechachanwate/Shutterstock, 71; UbjsP/Shutterstock, 72 (top); Jane McLoughlin/Shutterstock, 72 (bottom); Citysqwirl/iStock/Getty Images, 73; seven75/iStock/Getty Images, 74 (left); Chimperil59/iStock/Getty Images, 74 (right); OlyaSolodenko/iStock/Getty Images, 75 (left); Iva Vagnerova/Shutterstock, 75 (right); Siegfried Layda/The Image Bank/Getty Images, 76 (bottom); kschulze/iStock/Getty Images, 77 (left); IN Dancing Light/Shutterstock, 77 (right); constantgardener/iStock/Getty Images, 78 (bottom); Graeme L Scott/Shutterstock, 79 (top); Nadezhda Kharitonova/Shutterstock, 79 (bottom); Jeremy Christensen/iStock/Getty Images, 80; ReDunnLev/iStock/Getty Images, 81 (top); Danita Delimont/Shutterstock, 81 (bottom); Alena Vikhareva/iStock/Getty Images, 82; Grb/iStock/Getty Images, 86 (left); Dan4Earth/Shutterstock, 86 (right); Sundry Photography/iStock/Getty Images, 87; Studio 888/Shutterstock, 90 (left); cscredon/iStock/Getty Images, 90 (right); Baiploo/iStock/Getty Images, 91 (top); You Touch Pix of EuToch/Shutterstock, 91 (bottom); Sandi Smolker/iStock/Getty Images, 92, 94, 97; magicflute002/iStock/Getty Images, 93; AGabriel_Photo/Shutterstock, 96; Bawan Ari Purnawan/iStock/Getty Images, 98 (top); Stillgravity/Shutterstock, 98 (bottom), 112 (left); Francisco Blanco/iStock/Getty Images, 99; Vahan Abrahamyan/Shutterstock, 100; bgwalker/iStock/Getty Images, 101 (left); lindasky76/Shutterstock, 101 (right); Marina Poushkina/Shutterstock, 102 (bottom); ChiCasting/iStock/Getty Images, 103; kj2011/iStock/Getty Images, 104 (left); Greens and Blues/Shutterstock, 104 (right); JayL/Shutterstock, 105; LagunaticPhoto/iStock/Getty Images, 106 (left); Photo credit John Dreyer/Moment/Getty Images, 106 (right); Marbury/iStock/Getty Images, 107

**ABDOBOOKS.COM**
Published by Abdo Reference, a division of ABDO, PO Box 398166, Minneapolis, Minnesota 55439. 

Printed in China
102024
012025

Editor: Athena McGee
Series Designer: Colleen McLaren

**Library of Congress Control Number: 2024938383**
**Publisher's Cataloging-in-Publication Data**

Names: Hart, Rachel C., author.
Title: Poisonous and deadly plants / by Rachel C. Hart
Description: Minneapolis, Minnesota : Abdo Reference, 2025 | Series: North American field guides | Includes online resources and index.
Identifiers: ISBN 9781098296162 (lib. bdg.) | ISBN 9798384917168 (ebook)
Subjects: LCSH: Poisonous plants--Juvenile literature. | Toxins--Juvenile literature. | Dangerous plants--Juvenile literature. | Carnivorous plants--Juvenile literature. | Ecological science--Juvenile literature.
Classification: DDC 581.65--dc23